Field Guides to Finding a New Career

Advertising, Sales, and Marketing

The Field Guides to Finding a New Career series

Advertising, Sales, and Marketing

Arts and Entertainment

Education

Film and Television

Food and Culinary Arts

Health Care

Information Technology

Internet and Media

Nonprofits and Government

Outdoor Careers

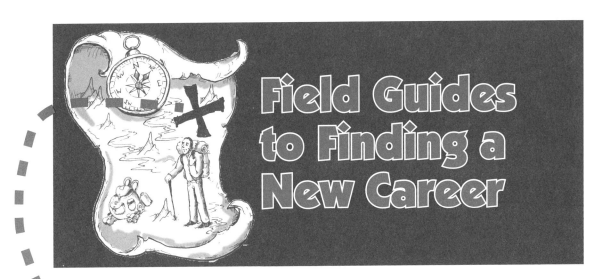

Field Guides to Finding a New Career

Advertising, Sales, and Marketing

By Ken Mondschein

Ferguson Publishing
An imprint of Infobase Publishing

Field Guides to Finding a New Career: Advertising, Sales, and Marketing

Ferguson
An imprint of Infobase Publishing
132 West 31st Street
New York, NY 10001

Library of Congress Cataloging-in-Publication Data

Mondschein, Ken.
    Advertising, sales, and marketing / by Ken Mondschein.
       p. cm.—(The Field guides to finding a new career series)
    Includes bibliographical references and index.
    ISBN-13: 978-0-8160-7596-6 (alk. paper)
    ISBN-10: 0-8160-7596-4 (alk. paper)
 1. Marketing—Vocational guidance—United States. 2. Advertising—Vocational
    guidance—United States. 3. Retail trade—Vocational guidance—United States.
    I. Title. HF5415.35.M66 2009
    658.80023'73—dc22

                                  2008043304

Ferguson books are available at special discounts when purchased in bulk quantities for businesses, associations, institutions, or sales promotions. Please call our Special Sales Department in New York at (212) 967-8800 or (800) 322-8755.

You can find Ferguson on the World Wide Web at http://www.fergpubco.com

Produced by Print Matters, Inc.
Text design by A Good Thing, Inc.
Illustrations by Molly Crabapple
Cover design by Takeshi Takahashi

Printed in the United States of America

Bang PMI 10 9 8 7 6 5 4 3 2 1

This book is printed on acid-free paper.

Contents

Introduction: Finding a New Career

Today, changing jobs is an accepted and normal part of life. In fact, according to the Bureau of Labor Statistics, Americans born between 1957 and 1964 held an average of 9.6 jobs from the ages of 18 to 36. The reasons for this are varied: To begin with, people live longer and healthier lives than they did in the past and accordingly have more years of active work life. However, the economy of the twenty-first century is in a state of constant and rapid change, and the workforce of the past does not always meet the needs of the future. Furthermore, fewer and fewer industries provide bonuses such as pensions and retirement health plans, which provide an incentive for staying with the same firm. Other workers experience epiphanies, spiritual growth, or various sorts of personal challenges that lead them to question the paths they have chosen.

Job instability is another prominent factor in the modern workplace. In the last five years, the United States has lost 2.6 *million jobs*; in 2005 alone, 370,000 workers were affected by mass layoffs. Moreover, because of new technology, changing labor markets, ageism, and a host of other factors, many educated, experienced professionals and skilled blue-collar workers have difficulty finding jobs in their former career tracks. Finally—and not just for women—the realities of juggling work and family life, coupled with economic necessity, often force radical revisions of career plans.

No matter how normal or accepted changing careers might be, however, the time of transition can also be a time of anxiety. Faced with the necessity of changing direction in the middle of their journey through life, many find themselves lost. Many career-changers find themselves asking questions such as: Where do I want to go from here? How do I get there? How do I prepare myself for the journey? Thankfully, the Field Guides to Finding a New Career are here to show the way. Using the language and visual style of a travel guide, we show you that reorienting yourself and reapplying your skills and knowledge to a new career is not an uphill slog, but an exciting journey of exploration. No matter whether you are in your twenties or close to retirement age, you can bravely set out to explore new paths and discover new vistas.

Though this series forms an organic whole, each volume is also designed to be a comprehensive, stand-alone, all-in-one guide to getting motivated, getting back on your feet, and getting back to work. We thoroughly discuss common issues such as going back to school, managing your household finances, putting your old skills to work in new situations, and selling yourself to potential employers. Each volume focuses on a broad career field, roughly grouped by Bureau of Labor Statistics' career clusters. Each chapter will focus on a particular career, suggesting new career paths suitable for an individual with that experience and training as well as practical issues involved in seeking and applying for a position.

Many times, the first question career-changers ask is, "Is this new path right for me?" Our self-assessment quiz, coupled with the career compasses at the beginning of each chapter, will help you to match your personal attributes to set you on the right track. Do you possess a storehouse of skilled knowledge? Are you the sort of person who puts others before yourself? Are you methodical and organized? Do you communicate effectively and clearly? Are you good at math? And how do you react to stress? All of these qualities contribute to career success—but they are not equally important in all jobs.

Many career-changers find working for themselves to be more hassle-free and rewarding than working for someone else. However, going at it alone, whether as a self-employed individual or a small-business owner, provides its own special set of challenges. Appendix A, "Going Solo: Starting Your Own Business," is designed to provide answers to many common questions and solutions to everyday problems, from income taxes to accounting to providing health insurance for yourself and your family.

For those who choose to work for someone else, how do you find a job, particularly when you have been out of the labor market for a while? Appendix B, "Outfitting Yourself for Career Success," is designed to answer these questions. It provides not only advice on résumé and self-presentation, but also the latest developments in looking for jobs, such as online resources, headhunters, and placement agencies. Additionally, it recommends how to explain an absence from the workforce to a potential employer.

Changing careers can be stressful, but it can also be a time of exciting personal growth and discovery. We hope that the Field Guides to Finding a New Career not only help you get your bearings in today's employment jungle, but set you on the path to personal fulfillment, happiness, and prosperity.

How to Use This Book

Career Compasses

Each chapter begins with a series of "career compasses" to help you get your bearings and determine if this job is right for you, based on your answers to the self-assessment quiz at the beginning of the book. Does it require a mathematical mindset? Communication skills? Organizational skills? If you're not a "people person," a job requiring you to interact with the public might not be right for you. On the other hand, your organizational skills might be just what are needed in the back office.

Destination

A brief overview, giving you and introduction to the career, briefly explaining what it is, its advantages, why it is so satisfying, its growth potential, and its income potential.

You Are Here

A self-assessment asking you to locate yourself on your journey. Are you working in a related field? Are you working in a field where some skills will transfer? Or are you doing something completely different? In each case, we suggest ways to reapply your skills, gain new ones, and launch yourself on your new career path.

Navigating the Terrain

To help you on your way, we have provided a handy map showing the stages in your journey to a new career. "Navigating the Terrain" will show you the road you need to follow to get where you are going. Since the answers are not the same for everyone and every career, we are sure to show how there are multiple ways to get to the same destination.

Organizing Your Expedition

Fleshing out "Navigating the Terrain," we give explicit directions on how to enter this new career: Decide on a destination, scout the terrain, and decide on a path that is right for you. Of course, the answers are not the same for everyone.

Landmarks

People have different needs at different ages. "Landmarks" presents advice specific to the concerns of each age demographic: early career (twenties), mid-career (thirties to forties), senior employees (fifties) and second-career starters (sixties). We address not only issues such as overcoming age discrimination, but also possible concerns of spouses and families (for instance, paying college tuition with reduced income) and keeping up with new technologies.

Essential Gear

Indispensable tips for career-changers on things such as gearing your résumé to a job in a new field, finding contacts and networking, obtaining further education and training, and how to gain experience in the new field.

Notes from the Field

Sometimes it is useful to consult with those who have gone before for insights and advice. "Notes from the Field" presents interviews with career-changers, presenting motivations and methods that you can identify with.

Further Resources

Finally, we give a list of "expedition outfitters" to provide you with further information and trade resources.

Make the Most of Your Journey

Perhaps no form of media today has as much effect on our lives as advertising. Ads come at us day and night, from magazines, newspapers, billboards, radio stations, television programs, cell phones, busses, trains, schools, and Web browsers. Products promise to make us youthful, cool, healthy, thin, and rich. To facilitate our purchases we are offered giveaways, rebates, free prizes, and discounts. Ads for political candidates and not-for-profits tell us who to vote for and what behaviors to avoid. In short, advertising tells us how we should measure status and what we should want out of life. Over $155 billion was spent on advertising in the United States alone in 2006, and $385 billion was spent worldwide—an amount expected to reach half a trillion dollars by 2010. As much creativity, hard work, money, and effort may go into a thirty-second commercial as an entire half-hour television program, and the talents who make and direct television commercials may go on to make feature films and become celebrities in their own right. With an influence, reach, and dollar value like this, it is only natural that creative people should feel drawn to the world of advertising.

Advertising is necessary for economic growth. Without advertising, businesses would have no way of getting the word out about their products. Thus, advertising is as old as economic activity itself. Ads can be traced as far back 4,000 B.C.E. The ancient Greeks made pottery that advertised its contents, and the Egyptians made papyrus posters for products. Medieval innkeepers hung up signs so even the illiterate knew there was ale to be had. Handbills became common after the invention of printing, and the industry took off in the nineteenth century when, in 1836, the French newspaper *La Presse* was able to lower its cover price by including advertising. Since women did most of the purchasing for the household, advertising was one of the first industries besides nursing and teaching in which women could find work. Movie product placements are almost as old as the industry itself: The first one is believed to be Hershey's chocolate in the 1927 Clara Bow film *Wings*. Finally, the invention of the powerful new media of radio and television led to new regulations, but also new opportunities—the possibilities of which began to be fully exploited as the 1960s made youth, energy, and creativity selling points. (For more on this, see Thomas Frank and Matt Weiland's terrific collection of essays, *Commodify Your Dissent*.)

The World Wide Web is a new frontier for advertising. From Google's ingenious AdSense algorithms to those annoying spam messages that clutter your inbox, every facet of the Web has been colonized by commercial messages. Some of this is certainly unwanted, but the fact is that running a Web site costs money. Revenue from advertising is what pays for most of your favorite Web sites and brings you needed content. Creating and selling ads on the World Wide Web is a new and profitable industry. At the same time, Internet advertising, using such things as social networking, behavioral targeting (that is, keeping track of your interests, based on what you click on), and contextual advertising (ads based on what you search for, such as Google's AdSense), can seem more like a modern social experiment than a way of making money. This brave new world, where advertising meets experimental, applied social science, can be discerned in such nontraditional practices as guerilla marketing—a hodge-podge of tricky techniques for planting information.

However, no form of media is also as misunderstood as advertising. It is far from the case that advertising is practiced by eccentric geniuses locked in their sky-high Madison Avenue creative laboratories. Most industry activity centers not on creating ads, but placing them. Only 40 percent of firms are involved in both the creation and placement of ads, while the remaining 60 percent work in one aspect of the business. Many of these specialize placing ads in one sort of media, such as radios, buses, or billboards. (Within the industry, only these sorts of shops are properly called "advertising agencies," though the term is often applied in a more general sense.)

Another misconception is that industry practice is limited to the powerhouses of New York City, Los Angeles, and San Francisco. Only 1 firm in 5 is located in New York State or California. That adds up to only one-quarter of all advertising workers. The idea that most people in advertising are employed by a huge agency is a myth as well. As of 2006, 70 percent of ad agencies in this country had five or fewer employees, according to the U.S. Bureau of Labor Statistics. The picture that emerges of the advertising industry is not an intimidating one, but rather one full of opportunities.

Entering the advertising world therefore poses both challenges and gratification for the career changer. On the plus side, there are infinite possibilities for the energetic and creative type of person, especially if this creativity is directed toward finding your own path. On the minus side, there are definite biases in the industry the young, hip, technologically savvy, and self-consciously avant-garde. The good news is that the farther you get from major metropolitan areas, the more room there is to breathe on your own terms and the less biases you encounter.

Still, working in advertising does not necessarily guarantee a creative career. In fact, coming up with the ads is only a small (but critical) part of the work. Placing the ads, either on the purchasing side or by selling space to media outlets, is another critical component. The core of sales management is quantification—as the saying goes, "You cannot manage what you cannot measure"—and so keeping track of metrics is also an important part of the advertising world. Things that marketing managers ask are: How effective are the ads? What does the public think about the product? How much name-recognition does the brand have? How are various marketing schemes such as rebates and bonuses working? (To do this, ad pros use special software and information-tracking systems.) Finally, recognize that advertising agencies, like all workplaces, also have need of accountants, human resources administrators, and assistants—positions that, while not as exciting as some others, can provide a bridge job to get you where you have to go.

All in all, several things define your options in the advertising world. The first is formal training. What degrees and certifications do you have? Those with backgrounds in statistics, demography, accounting, or other such mathematical disciplines are in demand for such careers as market analysts and market surveyors. Though you may have to retool and go back to school for additional training, your background gives you credibility in these departments. Those who majored in marketing are also well-placed, since marketing is at the heart of what advertising does. Managers and MBAs are in demand in all industries, especially on the sales side, though they may have to face the bias that only creative types are qualified to lead advertising agencies. Finally, fine artists, writers, and filmmakers with portfolios and a history of creative work have better chances of getting in on the creative side of things.

A second, and related, limiting factor is your previous experience. What have you been doing up to this point? Someone with a background in statistical demography will not find doing such work for an ad agency much different than doing it for a government bureaucracy. Likewise, a novelist might see similarities between writing fiction and writing ad copy. However, taking a step from surveys to the creative side of things might be a bit far to reach, or, conversely, from writing to running statistics-crunching programs. In this case you have several options: go back to school for additional education, take a bridge job to get you closer to where you want to be, work as an intern or in another voluntary capacity to gain valuable contacts and experience, or try to independently produce a body of work to show that you have the relevant skills. This may be a long-term project. The objective, much as in the games where you change one letter in a word to transform it into others, is to take logical steps to an ultimate goal.

Your geographical parameters are another factor. While it might seem that all the advertising jobs are on the coasts, the fact of the matter is that there may be more opportunities to break into the field right in your backyard. Not only is there less competition in heartland America, but also a greater opportunity to use your personal and professional connections where you are known best. (On the other hand, there are also fewer people, and, accordingly, less economic activity.) When you know your local market better than anyone else does, you have a definite "home field advantage" when starting your own business.

Finally, age is a factor. One thing that comes up again and again in insiders' discussions of the advertising world is its emphasis on youth and trendiness. Still, there are ways around this, and it is not an unbendable law for the entire advertising field. Though the creative end of the field prefers either the young and hip or else those with long, proven experience, it does not mean that advertising is closed to career changers. Those with a richness of experience in other fields must find a way to turn a liability into a strength. Make your past responsibility work for you. Look for similarities between what you do now and what you want to do, and emphasize those in your new career plan. One way to do this is to capitalize on your specific knowledge. A retired professor of sociology or demographics may be in demand to consult for a marketing agency, while a well-respected, retired senior executive can keep his or her hand in the game at trade shows. Those with management experience will need to parlay this into the world of advertising. Your challenge is always to find ways to make your experience relevant to the field—bearing in mind that "the field" includes many types of work.

Another option is starting your own business. The opportunities for this are myriad. To begin with, if you have the right connections, you can easily open a business buying and selling ad space in the media of your choice. If you have a statistics background, consider a demographic-analysis company. If you know the mail-order business, think about a direct-marketing firm. If you know an industry inside and out, you might represent it at trade shows. Likewise, if you have start-up capital and connections, consider opening a creative shop—even if you do not have any creative experience of your own, this is one way to get your foot in the door. Your only limiting factors are your potential client base, your creativity, and your capacity for hard work.

Advertising can be a fascinating, creative, rewarding field. It can also be intense, frustrating, cutthroat, arbitrary, crass, and hypocritical. Like everything else in the world, it is what you make of it. The keys to success are to know yourself and your talents, to carefully make your plan and follow it through, and to spend your social and financial capital wisely. Be flexible, be willing to be honest with yourself, and rest assured that, with this volume of the Field Guides to Finding a New Career in hand, you are well-equipped to make a go of it in the exciting world of advertising.

Self-Assessment Quiz

I: Relevant Knowledge

1. How many years of specialized training have you had?
   (a) None, it is not required
   (b) Several weeks to several months of training
   (c) A year-long course or other preparation
   (d) Years of preparation in graduate or professional school, or equivalent job experience

2. Would you consider training to obtain certification or other required credentials?
   (a) No
   (b) Yes, but only if it is legally mandated
   (c) Yes, but only if it is the industry standard
   (d) Yes, if it is helpful (even if not mandatory)

3. In terms of achieving success, how would rate the following qualities in order from least to most important?
   (a) ability, effort, preparation
   (b) ability, preparation, effort
   (c) preparation, ability, effort
   (d) preparation, effort, ability

4. How would you feel about keeping track of current developments in your field?
   (a) I prefer a field where very little changes
   (b) If there were a trade publication, I would like to keep current with that
   (c) I would be willing to regularly recertify my credentials or learn new systems
   (d) I would be willing to aggressively keep myself up-to-date in a field that changes constantly

5. For whatever reason, you have to train a bright young successor to do your job. How quickly will he or she pick it up?
    (a) Very quickly
    (b) He or she can pick up the necessary skills on the job
    (c) With the necessary training he or she should succeed with hard work and concentration
    (d) There is going to be a long breaking-in period—there is no substitute for experience

II: Caring

1. How would you react to the following statement: "Other people are the most important thing in the world?"
    (a) No! Me first!
    (b) I do not really like other people, but I do make time for them
    (c) Yes, but you have to look out for yourself first
    (d) Yes, to such a degree that I often neglect my own well-being

2. Who of the following is the best role model?
    (a) Ayn Rand
    (b) Napoléon Bonaparte
    (c) Bill Gates
    (d) Florence Nightingale

3. How do you feel about pets?
    (a) I do not like animals at all
    (b) Dogs and cats and such are OK, but not for me
    (c) I have a pet, or I wish I did
    (d) I have several pets, and caring for them occupies significant amounts of my time

4. Which of the following sets of professions seems most appealing to you?
    (a) business leader, lawyer, entrepreneur
    (b) politician, police officer, athletic coach
    (c) teacher, religious leader, counselor
    (d) nurse, firefighter, paramedic

5. How well would you have to know someone to give them $100 in a harsh but not life-threatening circumstance? It would have to be...
   (a) ...a close family member or friend (brother or sister, best friend)
   (b) ...a more distant friend or relation (second cousin, coworkers)
   (c) ...an acquaintance (a coworker, someone from a community organization or church)
   (d) ...a complete stranger

III: Organizational Skills

1. Do you create sub-folders to further categorize the items in your "Pictures" and "Documents" folders on your computer?
   (a) No
   (b) Yes, but I do not use them consistently
   (c) Yes, and I use them consistently
   (d) Yes, and I also do so with my e-mail and music library

2. How do you keep track of your personal finances?
   (a) I do not, and I am never quite sure how much money is in my checking account
   (b) I do not really, but I always check my online banking to make sure I have money
   (c) I am generally very good about budgeting and keeping track of my expenses, but sometimes I make mistakes
   (d) I do things such as meticulously balance my checkbook, fill out Excel spreadsheets of my monthly expenses, and file my receipts

3. Do you systematically order commonly used items in your kitchen?
   (a) My kitchen is a mess
   (b) I can generally find things when I need them
   (c) A place for everything, and everything in its place
   (d) Yes, I rigorously order my kitchen and do things like alphabetize spices and herbal teas

4. How do you do your laundry?
   (a) I cram it in any old way
   (b) I separate whites and colors

(c)   I separate whites and colors, plus whether it gets dried

(d)   Not only do I separate whites and colors and drying or non-drying, I organize things by type of clothes or some other system

5.   Can you work in clutter?
(a)   Yes, in fact I feel energized by the mess
(b)   A little clutter never hurt anyone
(c)   No, it drives me insane
(d)   Not only does my workspace need to be neat, so does that of everyone around me

IV: Communication Skills

1.   Do people ask you to speak up, not mumble, or repeat yourself?
(a)   All the time
(b)   Often
(c)   Sometimes
(d)   Never

2.   How do you feel about speaking in public?
(a)   It terrifies me
(b)   I can give a speech or presentation if I have to, but it is awkward
(c)   No problem!
(d)   I frequently give lectures and addresses, and I am very good at it

3.   What's the difference between *their, they're,* and *there*?
(a)   I do not know
(b)   I know there is a difference, but I make mistakes in usage
(c)   I know the difference, but I can not articulate it
(d)   *Their* is the third-person possessive, *they're* is a contraction for *they are,* and *there* is a deictic adverb meaning "in that place"

4.   Do you avoid writing long letters or e-mails because you are ashamed of your spelling, punctuation, and grammatical mistakes?
(a)   Yes
(b)   Yes, but I am either trying to improve or just do not care what people think

(c) The few mistakes I make are easily overlooked

(d) Save for the occasional typo, I do not ever make mistakes in usage

5. Which choice best characterizes the most challenging book you are willing to read in your spare time?

(a) I do not read

(b) Light fiction reading such as the Harry Potter series, *The Da Vinci Code*, or mass-market paperbacks

(c) Literary fiction or mass-market nonfiction such as history or biography

(d) Long treatises on technical, academic, or scientific subjects

V: Mathematical Skills

1. Do spreadsheets make you nervous?

(a) Yes, and I do not use them at all

(b) I can perform some simple tasks, but I feel that I should leave them to people who are better-qualified than myself

(c) I feel that I am a better-than-average spreadsheet user

(d) My job requires that I be very proficient with them

2. What is the highest level math class you have ever taken?

(a) I flunked high-school algebra

(b) Trigonometry or pre-calculus

(c) College calculus or statistics

(d) Advanced college mathematics

3. Would you rather make a presentation in words or using numbers and figures?

(a) Definitely in words

(b) In words, but I could throw in some simple figures and statistics if I had to

(c) I could strike a balance between the two

(d) Using numbers as much as possible; they are much more precise

4. Cover the answers below with a sheet of paper, and then solve the following word problem: Mary has been legally able to vote for exactly half her life. Her husband John is three years older than she. Next year,

their son Harvey will be exactly one-quarter of John's age. How old was Mary when Harvey was born?
(a) I couldn't work out the answer
(b) 25
(c) 26
(d) 27

5. Cover the answers below with a sheet of paper, and then solve the following word problem: There are seven children on a school bus. Each child has seven book bags. Each bag has seven big cats in it. Each cat has seven kittens. How many legs are there on the bus?
   (a) I couldn't work out the answer
   (b) 2,415
   (c) 16,821
   (d) 10,990

VI: Ability to Manage Stress

1. It is the end of the working day, you have 20 minutes to finish an hour-long job, and you are scheduled to pick up your children. Your supervisor asks you why you are not finished. You:
   (a) Have a panic attack
   (b) Frantically redouble your efforts
   (c) Calmly tell her you need more time, make arrangements to have someone else pick up the kids, and work on the project past closing time
   (d) Calmly tell her that you need more time to do it right and that you have to leave, or ask if you can release this flawed version tonight

2. When you are stressed, do you tend to:
   (a) Feel helpless, develop tightness in your chest, break out in cold sweats, or have other extreme, debilitating physiological symptoms?
   (b) Get irritable and develop a hair-trigger temper, drink too much, obsess over the problem, or exhibit other "normal" signs of stress?
   (c) Try to relax, keep your cool, and act as if there is no problem
   (d) Take deep, cleansing breaths and actively try to overcome the feelings of stress

3. The last time I was so angry or frazzled that I lost my composure was:
    (a) Last week or more recently
    (b) Last month
    (c) Over a year ago
    (d) So long ago I cannot remember

4. Which of the following describes you?
    (a) Stress is a major disruption in my life, people have spoken to me about my anger management issues, or I am on medication for my anxiety and stress
    (b) I get anxious and stressed out easily
    (c) Sometimes life can be a challenge, but you have to climb that mountain!
    (d) I am generally easygoing

5. What is your ideal vacation?
    (a) I do not take vacations; I feel my work life is too demanding
    (b) I would just like to be alone, with no one bothering me
    (c) I would like to do something not too demanding, like a cruise, with friends and family
    (d) I am an adventurer; I want to do exciting (or even dangerous) things and visit foreign lands

Scoring:

For each category…

For every answer of *a*, add zero points to your score.
For every answer of *b*, add ten points to your score.
For every answer of *c*, add fifteen points to your score.
For every answer of *d*, add twenty points to your score.

The result is your percentage in that category.

Advertising
Executive

Advertising Executive

Career Compasses

Here's the breakdown of what it takes to be a successful advertising executive.

Relevant Knowledge of the field (20%)

Caring about your clients' needs (20%)

Organizational Skills to handle the business side of multiple projects (20%)

Communication Skills to coordinate the different facets of a project, to run the creative team, and to develop effective advertising campaigns (40%)

Destination: Advertising Executive

The opinions people have of advertising professionals tend not to be neutral. The image of the advertising executive, or ad exec, in a Madison Avenue boardroom pitching brilliant national and international campaigns while millionaire CEOs listen to his or her every word may seem like the ultimate in attractive sophistication or simply a manipulative, purposeless way to earn a living. There may be truth in each, but it is important to understand that advertising is much more than this common popular conception.

All businesses, from multinational corporations to mom-and-pop stores, have to get the word out about their goods and services. What's more, not everything in advertising takes place in a big New York firm. Whereas some advertising executives work for ad agencies, many work in-house in larger corporations' advertising divisions, and many more work for small, regional companies that get the word out about local businesses. Additionally, the Internet has created exciting new markets and possibilities. With the advent of the World Wide Web, it has become increasingly necessary for ad execs to be technologically literate and in-the-know about recent trends and technologies. Some agencies even specialize in Web-based advertising. Executives in such agencies must be familiar with what the Internet-savvy community expects in its media.

Despite public perceptions, advertising executives do not always live in California or New York. In fact, only about 20 percent of firms and 25 percent of employees in the advertising industry live in these two states. Nor do they all work in huge agencies. The truth is that most people in advertising work in small businesses or "shops." Many are freelancers, self-employed, or own their own agencies. In 2006 7 of 10 of advertising agencies in the United States employed five or fewer employees, according to the U.S. Bureau of Labor Statistics. Nor is all the work creative. Many firms do not create ads but place them in magazines and newspapers, on radio and television, and in various other media. In fact, of the 48,000 advertising and marketing agencies that existed in the United States in 2006, only about 40 percent were the sort of full-service companies that handle all aspects of ads from creation to placement.

Thus, an advertising executive need not be in a creative line of work at all. He or she might be more interested in placement, marketing, or market research. Even an executive who gets to do creative work may spend more of his or her time on the mundane aspects of the job—particularly if it is a small business. This may make the job seem duller, but on the other hand, it also makes it easier to break into—especially if you have the right expertise in marketing, sales, or statistics.

Even an advertising executive who works in the creative end of things does more than merely dream up innovative and creative advertisements. An ad campaign requires a lot of planning, sifting through demographic information, and strategizing based on research. In addition to being responsible for creative materials, an advertising executive is responsible for market research (gathering information about competitors, the public you are selling to, and the market for your product), marketing strategy (how to achieve the greatest amount of sales with the best application of allotted resources), public relations (managing the flow of information about the company and the product to the public), promotion (including everything from cash-back incentives to co-branding and renaming athletic stadiums), placing the ads, pricing, and new product development based on information for the market.

Advertising is hard work. To begin with, the hours are long. Six-day, 80-hour weeks are not unusual in this high-powered career. Likewise, it is stressful. An advertising executive must be able to jump from one project to another while still paying attention to detail. Nor may he or she neglect the business side of the job. Expenses must be carefully detailed and campaigns meticulously planned. Despite all of this, the field is very competitive, with many people seeking positions every year. Though advertising is hard work, there are benefits, too. Not the least of these is financial. According to the Bureau of Labor Statistics, the median annual income for managers in the advertising field was $97,540!

Essential Gear

Expand your horizons. In today's global marketplace, advertising agencies are seeking people who can look beyond the regional or even national market. Showing your familiarity with foreign cultures and what appeals to them can only be a bonus. Emphasize your multicultural experience, travel history, language skills, or whatever else you can put to your advantage in reaching identifiable markets.

While advertising is an intensely competitive environment—it is been remarked that "friend" is a four-letter word—it also necessitates teamwork. While it is rewarding to have a good idea recognized, bad ones are also remembered, and the advertising world can be very cutthroat. There are also the necessities of trying to win business from competitors and appeasing demanding clients—and to avoid losing clients to rivals, or even those who have decided to leave your firm and set off on their own. Sometimes all you have to show for all the hard work is having convinced America to use one brand of toothpaste instead of the other—but how many people in the mass society accomplish anything close in their professional lives?

Advertising executives can come from many different backgrounds. Many advertising professionals have specialized degrees in the field.

Some employers prefer their advertising managers to have master's or MBA degrees, with an emphasis on marketing. On the other hand, others are promoted internally from within a company. Even if your undergraduate major fell outside the communications fields, you should be knowledgeable about marketing, consumer behavior, market research, sales, business law, and communication methods and media. A visual arts background, including knowledge of art history and photography, is also helpful. Computer skills are also necessary. Firms maintain all manner of purchasing and demographic data in databases, and knowing that you have the ability to use them is essential.

If your dream is to become an advertising executive, it is best to have a background in the necessary skill sets, even if not in the advertising industry itself. This is not a junior-level position, and it is definitely easier for those accustomed to some measure of responsibility to find employment. For some career changers, it may be necessary to go back to school to earn a master's or MBA with a concentration in advertising or marketing. Also, while it is easier to transfer in from a job that concentrates in marketing or public relations, all industries have need of advertising and promotions. Consider a bridge job in the field with which you are most familiar.

Starting your own agency is also a possibility. As noted above, many advertising executives work in small "shops" throughout the nation. What are the needs in your community? Ad creation? Placement? In this industry, forging your own destiny is sometimes the quickest way to the top. Enlist partners who will fill in your gaps, and understand that this will only work in underserved communities.

You Are Here

The path to becoming an advertising executive can begin from many different points.

Do you have a background in marketing, media, or other qualifications? Going into advertising can be a logical extension of something you have already done. Advertising blends creative endeavors and sound business sense. Remember that a large part of the advertising business consists not of making ads but of buying and selling placement for them. Moreover, if you have worked in fields such as marketing or media you may already have contacts with advertising agencies that would be willing to give you a chance. In this field more than credential-driven professions, allowances for deficient experience can be made on the basis of friendship and personality. Tailor your résumé to reflect the sorts of strengths that advertising agencies look for, especially your creative side.

Are you working in a similar specialized field? Though it is not as easy to transition to advertising from an unrelated field, career changers with specialized knowledge still have an advantage. A pharmaceutical executive or senior sales representative, for instance, might have the sort of hands-on experience with the legal technicalities of the marketplace that would prove helpful to a firm that specializes in drug advertising. An activist with a not-for-profit or a public-health worker might find a home in a firm that does public-health initiatives. Doing publicity for a candidate for public office might give you an "in" with a company that orchestrates political campaigns. Likewise, a former executive in a specialized field might find a home with an ad agency that creates materials for trade publications.

Essential Gear

Get online. The World Wide Web is an enormous boon to the advertising world. Not only does it provide a new media venue for getting the word out about your client's product or service, but ads can be directed at specific audiences. For this reason, it is important to get an idea of the lie of the virtual landscape. Read up on online advertising. You do not want to be caught flat-footed on the topic.

Note, however, that merely being creative or having a background in the arts is not enough to make it in advertising. There is an entire business side to the advertising world that is often lost in the glamorous image of being highly-paid for creative work.

Do you have no experience at all? You may want to consider going back to school for additional training. Note, however, that you will probably have to start at the bottom. To boost your résumé, you may also want to consider taking on some freelance assignments for local small enterprises or businesses run by friends and family. A portfolio can go a long way toward convincing an advertising agency to give you a shot. Likewise, it helps to consider a bridge job in the publicity or marketing departments of a company working in a field with which you are familiar. This is particularly true for older career changers.

Navigating the Terrain

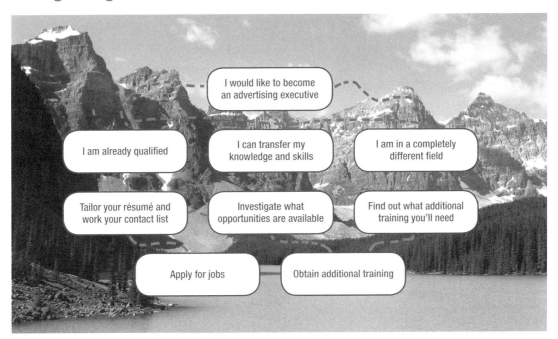

I would like to become an advertising executive

I am already qualified

I can transfer my knowledge and skills

I am in a completely different field

Tailor your résumé and work your contact list

Investigate what opportunities are available

Find out what additional training you'll need

Apply for jobs

Obtain additional training

Organizing Your Expedition

Before you set out, know where you are going.

Decide on a destination. Is your goal to be a top-level executive on Madison Avenue, planning national television, magazine, and radio campaigns? To work in a smaller, regional ad agency? To create materials for trade publications? To have a part-time business doing advertising for other local businesses? Keep in mind the highly competitive nature of the advertising world, as well as the fact that younger people tend to be preferred for entry-level positions while workers with more experience and a proven track record are more in demand for higher-level positions. Be realistic in your expectations. You may have the ideal résumé for that upper-level Madison Avenue job ad, but if you have a mortgage and children in school, you are not about to relocate to New York. If you are in your early twenties, you may be free to move, but an executive corner office is not in the cards for you any time soon. In both cases, you must

Stories from the Field
David Ogilvy, Advertising mogul

The man who did the most to make advertising what it is today was himself a career changer. David Ogilvy was born in Surrey, England, in 1911. Ogilvy inherited both financial sense and a hard work ethic from his Scottish Highlander father, who was a financial broker and a scholar of classical literature. However, his father's business was badly affected by the depression of the 1920s, and Ogilvy was only able to attend college on a scholarship. He left before earning his degree.

In his youth, Ogilvy tried his hand at different careers—as a chef in Paris, and, upon returning to England, as a door-to-door salesman of Aga-brand stoves. He was so successful at this that the company asked him to write a sales manual, which is still considered a classic of marketing. This book enabled Ogilvy's brother Francis to persuade his bosses at the London ad agency Mather and Crowther to give young David a try as an account executive.

After only a few months, Ogilvy had his big break. A potential client came into the offices of Mather and Crowther wishing to advertise his new hotel. Having only a tiny budget, he turned to the junior executive. Ogilvy's response was ingenious. He spent the entire budget on postcards, which he mailed out to everyone in the local telephone directory. On opening day, the hotel was filled with guests. This was Ogilvy's first experience with what is known as *direct advertising*, which he later called his "Secret Weapon." "I had tasted blood," Ogilvy later wrote of the experience in his *Confessions of an Advertising Man*—and he wanted more.

In 1938, Ogilvy moved to the United States to work for George Gallup's fledgling Audience Research Institute, where he helped improve upon the demographic innovator's statistical polling and research methods. In

match your goals with what's possible, whether it means shopping for work closer to home (perhaps with a smaller firm), or being willing to start at the bottom.

Scout the terrain. Look through classified ads on Web sites run by *Advertising Age* or the *New York Times* for jobs similar to the sort you would

World War II, he worked in the British Intelligence Service Office run out of their embassy in Washington, D.C. There he specialized in applying his knowledge to psychological warfare. After the war, he changed his career yet again, albeit in a completely new direction—he moved to Amish country in Lancaster, Pennsylvania, and tried his hand at farming for a few years.

In 1949 Ogilvy—having been a chef, salesman, researcher, spy, and farmer—returned to advertising. Together with the backing of two London firms and a bank balance of $6,000, he started what would become the renowned firm of Ogilvy, Benson, and Mather. Using his knowledge of human psychology and statistics, as well as his faith that successful advertising is based on knowledge of the consumer, Ogilvy spearheaded several hugely successful campaigns. The image of an aristocratic man with an eye-patch became "the man in the Hathaway shirt," and the bearded Commander Whitehead became "the man from Schweppes," both selling elegant Britishness to American consumers. Ogilvy informed Americans that the loudest noise that a Rolls-Royce makes at 60 miles per hour comes from the electric clock, and that Dove soap is the only brand with one-quarter moisturizing cream.

Though he retired to his château in France in 1973, Ogilvy returned to advertising in 1989 when the investment firm WPP acquired Ogilvy, Benson, and Mather for $864 million. Though relations between Ogilvy and Sir Martin Sorrell, WPP's owner, were acrimonious at first, the two men soon became friends. Ogilvy was named non-executive chairman of WPP, a post he held for three years. He died at his home in France in 1999 at the age of 88. His books *Ogilvy on Advertising* and *Confessions of an Advertising Man* are considered classics of the field and are still widely read today.

like to have. What qualifications do they ask of applicants? Do you have these qualifications or can you obtain them? Will you have to go back to school for additional education? Will you have to move to another city to find a job? If you need extensive training, you will have to take stock of your personal and financial situation. Do you have enough savings to be able to go back to school? Always take into account your life situation and that of those close to you. Also remember that you may need to modify your goals.

Find the path that's right for you. There are many paths to the advertising world, depending on what you want to do and what your background is. You may be stuck in an entry-level job for years, or you may simply need to pick up the phone and tell someone you are available. Remember to be flexible, and—especially if you are older—to go with your expertise rather than try to convince people you are something that you are not. It is a personality-driven field; falsity is commonplace, but self-doubt and fear are sniffed out quicker than a corpse. Keep it real, as it were.

Landmarks

If you are in your twenties . . . If you are part of "Generation Y," you are in luck. Not only is some amount of career searching expected at this age, but you are part of a much-desired demographic group. Advertisers not only want to know how you think and what your tastes are, but they are envious of your familiarity with new technology and eager to exploit the possibilities of the tools you use in everyday communications, such as social-networking Web sites. Just remember—if only to keep the senior players feeling important, you may have dues to pay. If you are right for the field, that may run about as long as your last health club membership.

If you are in your thirties or forties . . . Employees with some experience are welcome additions to advertising firms, especially if they are transferring from a related field. Your self-discipline and professional experience make you a much-desired commodity. The downside is that you may not have the background that advertising agencies look for. Be sure to emphasize parts of your background such as graphic design or demographic analysis that are key skills in the advertising world.

If you are in your fifties . . . At this age, you would be best off staying close to your original field. The aforementioned case of a pharmaceutical executive who goes to work for a pharmaceutical-advertising firm is a good example. Another is a petroleum executive who loans his expertise and knowledge of the market to an agency that has oil companies as clients. Scour your knowledge for any commercially applicable niche. If you are accomplished in several related disciplines and wise to current events, all the better—but for almost all entrants, it is best to dominate in one area first.

If you are over sixty . . . Though in many ways you are in the same boat as workers in their fifties, elder statesmen and stateswomen have some advantages of their own. Your seniority and experience make you a respected voice in your field. Be sure to capitalize on the wealth of your years by emphasizing problem-solving skills, leadership qualities, and your ability to see the big picture. If you are well-known in your community and have a solid reputation, you may succeed with your own small firm.

Further Resources

Advertising Age and *Adweek* are the industry's must-read trade journals for insider information and news. http://adage.com http://www.adweek.com

The Public Relations Society of America is the trade organization for public-relations professionals and individuals who work in advertising. http://www.prsa.org

The American Association of Advertising Agencies is the organization for agencies. http://www2.aaaa.org

Advertising
Creative Director

Advertising Creative Director

Career Compasses

Here's the breakdown of what it takes to become a creative director in an ad agency.

Relevant Knowledge—specifically, artistic talent and the "spark" that makes a good idea into a great idea (40%)

Caring about your clients' needs (20%)

Organizational Skills to direct multiple projects (20%)

Communication Skills to express your ideas (20%)

Destination: Advertising Creative Director

If an advertising executive is the brains of a firm, then the creative director is the heart. The job of the creative director is to oversee all the artistic aspects of the job, both written and visual materials, ensuring overall quality, making sure everything fits with what the client wants as well as the current state of the market. The first to be credited when a campaign goes right—and the first to be blamed when it does not—being a creative director holds a job that is at once demanding and rewarding. On the plus side, you get to see your ideas come to fruition and work in an intense, vibrant environment. However, the trade-offs are long hours and heavy responsibility.

Another of the pluses is monetary compensation. According to the U.S. Bureau of Labor Statistics, median annual earnings for managers in advertising and promotions were $73,060 in May of 2006. About.com lists salaries of between $62,798 and $115,526 for creative directors with five years' experience, and salaries can occasionally reach over $200,000 for those at the top of their field. Note, however, that these are the salaries for very senior creative directors. As someone just coming into the field—and who will likely have to work his or her way up in the world—you will likely be earning quite a bit less.

Essential Gear

Design brief or creative brief. A design brief or a creative brief is the résumé of an advertising project, detailing who, what, when, where, why, and how. It not only sums up the proposed plan of action for the client, but gives the creative personnel executing the plan a clear course of action. It also helps all involved get their "ducks in a row," outlining expectations and methods used. A design brief tends to be similar to a creative brief, but contains more business information such as budgets.

Thankfully, there are lots of opportunities in the advertising world. For instance, it is not the case that all creative directors have to live in Los Angeles or New York City. Though it is a common myth that New York's Madison Avenue is the heart of the advertising world, and that everyone who works in film or TV, including commercials, lives in Hollywood, the truth is that only one in five advertising firms and a quarter of all advertising employees are located in California or New York State. Seven in 10 firms, in fact, had five or fewer employees in 2006. Small advertising firms are found throughout the nation, though the coasts are arguably the artistic and creative centers. See what is available in your neighborhood, and remember that going out on your own is always a possibility. Note also that the goals and approaches of a creative director may vary widely between larger and smaller firms. What is described here is the way the job is practiced by the larger agencies.

Generally, creative directors in advertising agencies come in two flavors—those with backgrounds in visual media, and those with backgrounds in copywriting. Despite this, the dual nature of the job means that those from literary backgrounds must also have an eye for composition and design, and those from artistic backgrounds must also have an ear for the music of language. Creative directors tend to be promoted from within the ranks, graduating from junior to more senior positions. However, nontraditional career paths are also possible. Career changers with backgrounds in visual arts or writing are well-positioned to find themselves in the creative department of an advertising firm. There is no universal set of qualifications for becoming a creative director, a position that David Ogilvy, "the father of advertising," once described as "trumpeter swans." The most relevant qualification is creativity and the ability to come up with good ideas—an alchemy that is extremely difficult to master, but which is more precious than gold.

The job is also a very political one. The creative director must mediate between the clients' wishes, the agency's management, and the often-idiosyncratic visions of their staff. The artistic process is not always a linear one, but it must be made to fit a business model. At the same time as he or she maintains an artistic flair and a penchant for creative, out-of-the box ideas, the creative director must also stay disciplined and think of the bottom line. Creative directors with a flair for business can find themselves at the very top of the food chain. In the advertising world, there is a definite bias that only "creative" types can lead—a bias that works in creative directors' favor.

Software skills are also a necessity. A whole range of computer programs, particularly Adobe's graphics and photo-editing software, Illustrator and Photoshop, are standard tools of the trade. You will need to know QuarkXpress for laying out text and Microsoft Office Suite's PowerPoint for making client presentations. Finally, you will need to be familiar with online media and how it is created, particularly Adobe's Flash graphics program. If you do not already have proficiency in these programs, consider taking courses or even buying them for yourself and tinkering with them. Most commercial artists who you will be working with have used them for years, and it is handy to know what can and ca not be done with these tools.

For people turned off by the advertising profession's culture yet who have a knack for persuasion, there are still options available. Many campaigns are targeted toward steering people *away* from certain consumer behaviors (such as buying cigarettes), or seek to raise awareness of a social or political cause—or even take aim at consumerism itself (see

"Adbusters" in the Further Resources section for an example of this). Thus, even countercultural career changers who would not seem drawn to advertising might find themselves filling the role of creative director.

You Are Here

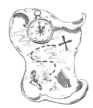

Your journey toward becoming an advertising creative director can begin from several places.

Do you have a background in art, writing, film, or other related occupations? The advertising world wants you! Your expertise as a writer, filmmaker, graphic designer, or other sort of creative professional may be just the ticket you need to get your foot in the door of the advertising world. Be prepared, however. You may need to work in a lower-level position for a while before you are given a position of responsibility. Creative directors are typically required to have five to seven years of advertising experience.

Are you working in a similar specialized field? There is probably a niche in advertising for you. Be creative. Workers in software or Web development can easily cross over to doing creative work for an ad agency. Emphasize your strengths and apply for jobs that play to your already-established skills. (You will probably need to take a bridge job in the art or copywriting departments.) Again, creative director is a final destination on the distant horizon, not a nearby rest stop.

Essential Gear

Awards. Industry awards are not only recognition for the work you've done, but also—whether fairly or unfairly—perhaps the single most important criteria by which creative personnel are judged. Industry groups give out annual awards in a variety of advertising media.

Are you coming in from the cold? Do not worry! Many agencies find that their most valuable employees are those with life experience. Your outside training and qualifications can be an asset. This is particularly true of those who might know a certain market particularly well. You may have to find a bridge job, such as writing copy for trade magazines, that will enable you to develop a portfolio and gradually work your way toward the advertising world. While you may have to start at the bottom, remember that there is no set course of training for creative individuals and that getting there is half the fun.

Navigating the Terrain

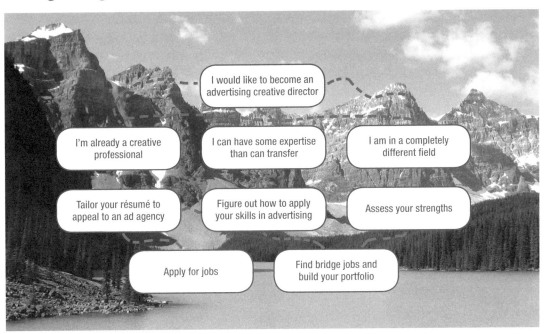

I would like to become an advertising creative director

I'm already a creative professional

I can have some expertise than can transfer

I am in a completely different field

Tailor your résumé to appeal to an ad agency

Figure out how to apply your skills in advertising

Assess your strengths

Apply for jobs

Find bridge jobs and build your portfolio

Organizing Your Expedition

Before you set out, know where you are going.

Decide on a destination. Obviously, you want to find a way to earn a living with your creativity. But be flexible! Advertising agencies rarely hire creative directors without lots of experience. Decide if your path to the top will be through the copywriting side or the graphic-arts side— or perhaps through Internet technologies. The first step is to figure out where your talents lie. Is your talent with words or images? What qualifications and experience do you need to get a foot in the door? What

Notes from the Field

Rose Samuelson
Advertising creative director
New York, New York

What were you doing before you decided to change careers?

I changed careers a number of times. I went to school for biology, worked after college as a writer and editor at a newspaper, then transitioned into editorial design and graphic design.

Why did you change your career?

I was looking for the right fit.

How did you make the transition?

For each transition I took bridge jobs that played off skills I previously had but added something new. For example, after college I marketed myself as a science writer to break into reporting. I learned editorial design as an editor and used that to get a job at a newsprint magazine and ad agency.

There were some rough patches when I took a variety of service and office jobs. I applied for a lot of jobs and got rejected a lot. I kept myself busy learning graphic design programs. I was worried that I would have to do a lot of explaining about my résumé. What I have learned is that most people care about your portfolio and attitude more.

What are the keys to success in your new career?

The biggest key to success is that it is a good fit for me so I am motivated to give it my all.

can you do to build up your portfolio—which is perhaps the single most important thing that decides if an ad agency will hire you as part of the creative team? (See the chapters on advertising copywriters and graphic designers for more on entering these career tracks.) Also consider if there is a nontraditional career path open to you, such as through fact-checking technical advertisements or through Internet or viral marketing projects.

Scout the terrain. Generally speaking, creative directors are required to lead a diverse, creative team; meet with clients; keep the project on schedule; and, of course, come up with winning ideas. As you progress in your career in advertising, you will need to emphasize your managerial skill as well as your creative side. Make a two-column list. On the left-hand side, write everything in your background that a creative director should have. On the right-hand side, write the things you lack. Prioritize them, and come up with a concrete plan and time frame to fulfill each one. (This is, incidentally, a good exercise to follow with any career-change.)

Find the path that's right for you. While academic credentials are not everything, do not write off the possibility of going back to school to bolster your résumé. Chemists or English majors might be able to play on their technical knowledge of pharmaceuticals or their ability to craft a phrase, but they might find a degree in art or advertising will further boost their credentials. A lot of advertising is market analysis. Being able to show how your pitch will hit the needed demographics (something you would learn with an advertising degree or MBA with an emphasis in advertising) might be the difference between success and failure. Finally, remember that no one will hire you as a creative director off the bat. This job is a long-term goal that you will come to after many years of success in another creative endeavor in advertising.

Landmarks

If you are in your twenties . . . Not only are young people seen as more creative, but they are considered more in tune with pop culture. If you want to know what the latest trends are in fashion or music, ask a twenty-something. Younger people are also seen as more adept with technology. The downside is that no one thinks of you as particularly responsible. Do not be in a rush. Build your résumé through a bridge job, always keeping your end goal in sight. This is also the perfect time to consider going back to school.

If you are in your thirties or forties . . . In many ways, mid-career changers are at the top of their game. Not only are you at a mature and responsible stage of your life, but you know what consumers with the most disposable income want. If you already have a background in creative media, you are in an especially good position to change to advertising. However, one of your biggest challenges is not to seem so out-of-touch and settled that you will not fit into the creative side of the advertising world. A touch of rebellion is a good thing. You should also make it clear that your "adult" life will not be an obstacle to working long hours.

If you are in your fifties . . . While your life experience might be a valuable asset, this is also a difficult time to change careers. In this case, it is best if you are already well-established in a field that is closely related to advertising. Regardless, make the most of your related experience. If you live an underserved locality and are willing to hustle and learn on the go, you may set up a small shop in your community—especially if you are already personally popular. See what opportunities and needs exist in your neighborhood.

If you are over sixty . . . At this point, it can be difficult to change careers. advertising is not, on the other hand, necessarily a young person's game. The voices of experienced professionals from other fields might be especially welcomed in advertising agencies dealing with those specific audiences. For instance, a former executive at a tire company might consult with an agency that handles tire advertising.

Further Resources

Advertising Age and *Adweek* are the industry's must-read trade journals. http://adage.com http://www.adweek.com
The Public Relations Society of America is the trade organization for public-relations professionals and individuals who work in advertising. http://www.prsa.org
Adbusters gives a good counterpoint to the world of consumerism. http://www.adbusters.org

Sales Representative

Sales Representative

Career Compasses

Here's the breakdown of what it takes to become an advertising sales representative.

Relevant Knowledge of the market and/or the product you are selling (20%)

Caring about what your customers need. Caring is the source of "people skills"—an essential qualification for this job (10%)

Organizational Skills to keep track of records and invoices (10%)

Communication Skills to make the sale (60%)

Destination: Sales Representative

Advertising sales representatives are vital to the functioning of many media ventures. Newspapers, television, radio, and many Web sites all run on selling advertisements. The sales representatives who work for these companies to solicit these placements are called *inside agents*. Many sales representatives also work for advertising agencies, soliciting outside firms to place the ads made by the creative department. These are known as *outside agents*. These sales representatives are the ad agency's troops on the ground, the soldiers who place the actual advertisements. Some also work for firms that specialize in selling ad space. This is not to say, however, that being an advertising sales representative is in any way a low-status job. Sales representatives are a vital part of the overall selling strategy, and their day-to-day interactions with customers not only help spread awareness of products and services among the public but also give vital feedback as to how the product is doing.

This career is perhaps the most common in the advertising industry. Fully 63 percent of people working in advertising are sales representatives. While the U.S. Bureau of Labor Statistics 2006 figures indicate that about a tenth of the people in advertising were self-employed (458,000 of all advertising workers were salary workers while 46,800 were self-employed), sales representatives tend to number among those employed by others. Their job, after all, is not autonomous—they can only function as part of a larger organism. Advertising sales representatives are found all over the country. More than half of advertising sales representatives work in the information sector, mainly in media outlets such as television and radio that make their money from selling advertising space.

Essential Gear

Inside agent or outside agent. This is the great division in advertising sales. *Inside agents* work for media companies and approach, or are approached by, potential advertisers. Being an *outside agent* can be easier, since your job is to approach media outlets to find venues in which to place your company's advertisements. Outside agents may work for PR firms, advertising agencies, or directly for the providers of goods and services.

An advertising sales representative's most important attribute is his or her personality. After all, most contact with clients is person-to-person, whether on the phone or in a face-to-face meeting. Thus it is important to be friendly, charismatic, and outgoing, while always maintaining a professional demeanor. Though a sales representative might find him- or herself working the phones most of the time, there are many other interactions at meetings, business conferences, and lunches. This is especially true when working with larger clients. A good sales representative knows how to pinpoint sales opportunities, whether it is by attending industry trade shows or seeking introductions to other people through his or her network.

Communication skills are important to be able to work out all the nuances of a deal. What are the rates? How much money is going to change hands? Where will the spots be placed? Will any "extras" be added on? Is there a discount for bulk buys? A good sales representative is creative and innovative in finding new sales opportunities. For instance, a radio station may broker a hard deal in which an agency pays dearly for airtime—but a good sales representative will try to arrange for the DJs on the morning drive-time show to mention the product every day.

Furthermore, an advertising sales representative must be organized. Most handle multiple accounts and contacts. Keeping these straight is essential. It is important to know what money is going where, and who owes you what. Maintaining a list of contacts, meanwhile, is simply good sales strategy. It tells you who you have already approached, who you will approach in the future, and any details that might help you make the sale. In the past this used to be called your "Rolodex," but these days it is just as likely to be electronic.

Essential Gear

Cold call. "Cold calling" is advertising parlance for when an inside agent solicits business from previously unknown parties, rather than having them come to her. This can be a fine entry-level job if you are in your early twenties, but because of the overwhelming majority of people you will call, it tends to be heavy on workload and light on rewards. The exception to this is if you are dealing with a small market. For instance, there are only so many people who buy dental drills; a new journal for dentists will definitely perk up the interests of dental-drill manufacturers.

An important addition to the sales representative's arsenal is "viral marketing." Many people working as sales representatives in modern ad agencies might not sell ad space at all but rather orchestrate creative and innovative campaigns to insert their message into the public consciousness. The attractive young woman you hear loudly requesting a certain brand of gin be used in her martini, the slogans written in chalk all over the busy downtown area, or the brightly-painted convertibles filled with model-perfect young people handing out free samples might all be part of these campaigns.

Another innovation is selling on the Internet. The online world does some things differently from the brick-and-mortar industries. For instance, rather than selling magazine pages or billboards, a Web site might sell part of the space on its pages for a certain amount of time, a certain number of page views (that is, the number of times the ad is loaded), or choose to be paid on "click-throughs"—people who click on the ad to see what it is all about. While a good portion of online advertising sales are done through automated systems such as Google's AdWords, there is still a high degree of human involvement in the process. For instance, Mike Falcone (see "Notes from the Field" below) works for the Internet news aggregator Fark.com. This is a popular Web site that posts amusing news stories and allows users to comment on them. It is very widely read among 18-to-35-year-olds, many of whom work in technical industries and/or have interests in such subjects as science fiction, travel, and microbrewing. Falcone accordingly targets his sales efforts to television networks that have science-fiction shows or to microbreweries. Since Fark is also a very well-known site, Falcone often has potential advertisers approach him. Part of the job is cutting deals with advertisers, which makes selling advertising space on the Internet not that much different from traditional advertising sales.

For an inside agent, the first step in selling advertising space—even before the initial contact—is to do your homework. What are the potential client's needs? What are their products or services? Who are their current and potential customers? To what market segment, demographic, or geographical area do they sell? This essential information grounds your initial meeting. This way, you can show exactly how your media plan can help move their product. Your research goes into an advertising proposal detailing objectives and methods of your plan, including specifics of market coverage and demographics, cost, and perhaps some sample ads. If a deal is made, the sales agent continues to act as the client's main point of reference, relaying needs and concerns and helping to develop the campaign and the advertisements. This may include anything from receiving the ad's data files from the advertising agency to helping a client tape a radio spot. Sales agents also handle invoicing and tracking payments.

An outside agent has a similar task, albeit from the opposite end. After reviewing the client's needs and researching appropriate media outlets, the outside agent will present a list of potential places to advertise. He or she will then approach the media outlets to broker deals, negotiate prices, and attempt to get the best value possible for their clients. This job requires a good knowledge of the media marketplace, as well as what demographics consume what media.

A sales representative's compensation can vary widely, as it usually includes commissions on ads placed. As of 2006, the median annual income for an advertising sales agent was $42,750. The top half made between $29,450 and $63,000 with the lowest 10 percent earning $21,460. However, the highest 10 percent of the profession earned more than $91,280 a year. Those in the motion picture industry made the most, while those in publishing, including newspapers, made the least. Though the print industry is shrinking as local newspapers become increasingly consolidated, online advertising is taking up much of the slack and expanding the opportunities for selling advertising.

The work environment for an advertising sales representative can be intense because there is pressure to constantly be productive. However, there is a definite cycle of activity based on the rhythm of the ad campaign or the production schedule. Your success depends on how much you sell, and hours are often long and irregular. One advantage is that you can work at home. This is particularly true for Internet sales. While there is no specialized educational path to becoming a sales representative, necessary skills include the ability to work with people and to research what the market wants. You need to find out as much about potential clients as you can, including how you can suit their needs, and maintain a productive relationship with them. Additional duties include keeping records of accounts, analyzing and reporting on demographics, and helping to plan campaigns. For this, organizational skills are essential.

Transitioning to the sales representative job is easier than for many other positions in advertising. Emphasize your communication skills—by example, not braggadocio—as well as sales experience and familiarity with the local media landscape. Sales reps are the majority of ad employees, and they are the ones who bring in the money. If you can do this, do not be shy. You are the lifeblood. Senior employees may aim to

Essential Gear

Multilingualism. Being able to speak a second language is a definite plus. Many media and advertisers, especially those serving Spanish-language market or an international audience, are part of larger, English-speaking businesses. There are also foreign-owned companies that do business in the United States. The ability to translate between the two audiences can be a big advantage.

become supervisors. Senior sales representatives with the requisite education, training, and experience are well-situated to become marketing managers, as outlined in the next chapter.

You Are Here

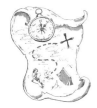

You can take your first steps toward becoming a sales representative from a variety of paths.

Are you already working in sales? Then you are well-placed to tailor your résumé to become an advertising sales representative. Again, emphasize your people skills, sales experience, and organizational abilities. Your job will involve skilful negotiations on the phone with media buyers for magazines, newspapers, television and radio stations, and other such businesses. A pleasant phone manner and a system to keep track of leads will prove invaluable.

Are you an expert in a particular field? Specialized professions, such as pharmaceuticals, have specialized requirements. It is helpful to know who are the "players" in a particular field. If you are transitioning out of one of these fields and looking for other work, you are particularly well-placed to move into a career selling advertisements to (and for) in-trade journals and other industry-specific publications. Emphasize your knowledge of the field and your understanding of the buyers. Use your experience to position yourself as a seller, even if you plan eventually to move onto a different sales niche. If it makes your blood run cold to sell to your former field, know that before you try. On the other hand, if you cannot sell to your old field, it could be that selling ad space is not for you.

Are you making a "cold call?" The good news is that because most learning in this career is on-the-job, you can transition into advertising sales from almost anywhere. Be creative, and show potential employers how you can be an asset to their businesses. You may also want to concentrate on working for, and with, small businesses, whether local or online. Be forewarned, however, that you may have to start at the bottom.

Navigating the Terrain

I'd like to become an advertising sales representative

Look at ads for jobs you might like

See how much of your experience applies

Tailor your résumé

Apply for jobs

Organizing Your Expedition

Before you set out, know where you are going.

Decide on a destination. So, you want to become an advertising sales representative. This an excellent career choice: Because of the anticipated growth in this field and the expansion of new media outlets, many new sales representatives will be needed in coming years.

Scout the terrain. Look at classified ads for jobs you might like to land. What skills do you possess that might transfer? Alternatively, be creative and take charge! Do you know anyone with a business who might need someone to buy (or sell) advertising? That is what Mike Falcone (see "Notes from the Field," below) did.

Find the path that's right for you. Tailor your résumé to reflect your strengths. While academic credentials are not the most important thing

Notes from the Field
Mike Falcone,
Advertising sales representative
New York, New York

What were you doing before you decided to change careers?

I was an elevator salesman. It had its ups and downs, but it was mostly down.

Why did you change your career?

I really, really hated being an elevator salesman.

How did you make the transition?

It is a case of knowing the right person at the right time. In my case, I knew Drew Curtis, the founder for the Internet news aggregator Fark.com. I spoke to Drew and it happened that he needed a guy to sell ads for the site.

What are the keys to success in your new career?

The understanding of a client's goals and how I can hone in and effectively hit their goals. You also have to be proactive. Speaking of which, if anyone reading this wants to reach a few million people in the 18-to-35-year-old demographic.

in this career choice, people skills are. Your biggest helper will be previous experience in sales. Specialized knowledge of a particular field is also a plus, particularly if it is a high-value, prestigious industry.

Landmarks

If you are in your twenties . . . This is an excellent time to get into advertising sales. Your youth and flexibility will work for you as you learn the ropes and work your way up the chain to positions of more and more responsibility. The important thing here is to make sure you do not get stuck in "dead-end jobs," endlessly cajoling local businesses into advertising with your local newspaper (though two years of that can be great experience).

If you are in your thirties or forties . . . While you might be frustrated at the idea of starting from the bottom (and potential employers might consider you too old for entry-level positions), conversely, as a mid-career changer, you might be able to parlay your experience into a supervisory position. For instance, if you are used to complex negotiations, then you might have the expertise needed to negotiate packages from media buyers for a large ad agency.

If you are in your fifties . . . A senior career changer, especially one with years of experience in a specialized field, can be a valuable asset to advertising agencies and media outlets that serve that industry. Make your years of experience count for you!

If you are over sixty . . . Much as with career changers in their fifties, a senior, respected worker can capitalize on his or her long years of experience. Conversely, advertising sales can also be a great part-time second career after your formal "retirement." It can keep you involved with people and with different branches of the local media landscape.

Further Resources

Advertising Age and *Adweek* are the industry's must-read trade journals. http://adage.com   http://www.adweek.com
The Newspaper Association of America has want-ads for advertising sales representatives, as well as industry news. http://www.naa.org

Marketing Manager

Marketing Manager

Career Compasses

Here's the breakdown of what it takes to become a marketing manager.

Relevant Knowledge—you have to know your product, as well as the marketplace (20%)

Caring about your clients and your company (10%)

Organizational Skills to keep your team on-track and to manage accounts (50%)

Communication Skills to effectively get across goals and needs (20%)

Destination: Marketing Manager

Marketing managers, in the words of Philip Kotler and Kevin Lane Keller's 2006 textbook *Marketing Management*, practice "the art and science of choosing target markets and getting, keeping and growing customers through creating, delivering, and communicating superior customer value." In other words, they apply the modern principles of marketing, such as targeting demographics and creating brand identity; choosing the audience, timing, and the vectors of their message; and, of course, managing these efforts by analyzing and quantifying their results. Marketing managers are thus responsible not only for marketing strategy, but also for research, strategic planning, pricing, selling and purchasing advertising space, organizing promotions, and maintaining public relations. Theirs are some of the most comprehensive positions in the advertising, sales, and marketing industry.

Other than this, the job description can vary widely. A marketing manager for a bank might get the word out on new financial products, while the marketing manager for an opera house might keep in touch with subscribers and promote events. The exact nature of the task might also depend on the company. In a small firm, you might be responsible for all parts of the job description, while marketing managers for a large corporation might each be responsible for one subfield in particular, such as public relations. For the purposes of this chapter, consider marketing manager as a single career covering all aspects of the job.

So, what are the parts of a marketing manager's job? To answer this, we first need to ask, "What is marketing?" Plainly put, marketing is the science of promoting trade. It incorporates advertising, distribution, and selling. It also involves measuring results and anticipating future market needs. Its basis is the "Four P's": product, price, place, and promotion (see "Essential Gear"). In this, it can take into account everything from package design to the architecture of the sales space.

Demographic analysis is another part of the marketing manager's job. Quite simply, this is finding out who might buy your products or use your services so that marketing can be more effectively targeted. Who is in the market? Men? Women? Teenagers? Homeowners? While men might be more inclined to buy a heavy-duty pickup truck, women are the traditional audience for dish soap. How do you reach them—and at what cost does your pitch justify a premium buy? Teenagers might be impressed with a new line of casual clothing, while homeowners will be in the market for

Essential Gear

The Five Cs. In order to market something effectively, you need to know the who, what, when, where, why, and how. Marketing managers break this down into five categories: customer analysis (who you are selling to), company analysis (who you are), collaborator analysis (who is working with you), competitor analysis (what you are up against), and analysis of the industry context (including such details of demand for your products).

flood insurance. However, marketing can get much more complex than these simple questions. What geographic region do they lie in? You are not going to get much mileage advertising hurricane insurance in Maine, and while suburban soccer moms might like a new fuel-efficient hybrid SUV, they might not be too inclined to buy their kids T-shirts featuring the faces of deceased revolutionaries. What values do consumers associate with the product? Is it cool, like name-brand sunglasses? Safe, like the aforesaid homeowner's insurance? Rebellious, like a T-shirt stenciled with a Marxist gueril-la's iconic portrait? Finally, how do you reach your target market? Where do they hang out? What sort of TV shows do they watch? It is this sort of analysis that gives you an idea of how to most effectively spend each precious marketing dollar. It is also in this region that a marketing manager's job might overlap with that of a market research analyst.

Essential Gear

Marketing strategy. Who are you going to sell to? Why do they want your products? What idea or concept do customers associate your product with? How do you implant this idea in their heads? The answers to these and other questions guide the creation of a marketing strategy. After deciding on your "Five C" strategy, you need to implement it with the market-er's "Four P's": product management (the overall view), pricing (how much it costs), place (where it is going to be sold and how it gets there), and promotion.

Another part of the marketing manager's job is conducting market research. This goes both ways: The marketer usually wants to find out how the public perceives the product, as well as anticipate their future wants and needs. There are a number of ways of doing this. Sometimes, information is collected via direct questionnaires that may be incorpo-rated into the packaging materials, sent by e-mail or post, or taken by telephone surveyors. Other times, marketers will assemble focus groups, contract with polling organizations, or even interview people on the street.

Next, how do you communicate your message to the people in your target market? We are all familiar with some of the more intrusive means of marketing—direct mail, also known as junk mail (but its aim is getting better); telemarketers (who call during dinner), and pop-up ads on the Internet (which we download pop-up blockers to stop). Likewise, we have gotten very good at ignoring the more traditional types of advertising, such as television spots, billboards, and bus ads—even as every person older than two distinguishes between the obnoxious and the clever, pleasing, or humorous ads. Still, modern marketers have therefore developed a number of nontraditional tools to circumvent these things. One is *viral marketing*, which seeks to engineer a catchy idea and inject it quickly into the cultural bloodstream. An example of this is the 2006 movie *Snakes on a Plane*, which unexpectedly caught fire on the Internet despite (or rather because of) its ludicrous concept. Another is *experiential marketing*, in which people actually go to the marketers—for a brand-sponsored concert, for instance—and are exposed to the marketing material via innovative methods such as audiovisual displays and simulations. The aim is to make the potential consumer feel personally connected to the brand. Similarly, the U.S. Army brings Humvees to shopping malls to help get potential recruits interested.

A marketing manager ideally has a background in business administration, demographics, advertising, or a related field. Essential marketing manager skills are creativity, computer skills, and, of course, communication skills. Depending on the industry, certification might be desirable. For instance, the Public Relations Society of America offers certification for experienced PR professionals. Because of the demands of the field, marketing managers tend to be promoted from junior roles, often internally within a company—though this should not discourage the determined career changer. Those who are working in advertising, promotions, public relations, or sales are in particularly strong positions to transfer to this field.

Essential Gear

Meme. According to the scientist Richard Dawkins, "[A]ll life evolves by the differential survival of replicating entities... I think that a new kind of replicator has recently emerged... It is still in its infancy, still drifting clumsily about in its primeval soup, but already it is achieving evolutionary change at a rate that leaves the old gene panting far behind. The new soup is the soup of human culture." The "new replicator" Dawkins speaks of is the *meme*, a neologism he coined by analogy to "gene." A meme, quite simply, is a mind-virus. It is a snippet of information, whether a technique for making stone tools or the tune of an advertising jingle, that gets passed from mind to mind. The Holy Grail of modern advertising is to create a meme so infectious that people will rush out to buy the product. Unfortunately, just as we cannot create life, we cannot "force" a meme into circulation.

According to the U.S. Bureau of Labor Statistics, 167,000 Americans identified themselves as marketing managers in 2006. Though the marketing manager field is expected to experience average growth, be warned. Competition for choice positions is intense. Like all jobs at the top, the work environment can be stressful and the hours long. The job also may require significant amounts of travel, especially meeting with clients and traveling to attend industry association events. However, marketing managers are richly rewarded: According to the U.S. Bureau of Labor Statistics, their median annual salary was $98,720 in 2006. Because of their highly public role, marketing managers' potential for promotion is almost unlimited.

You Are Here

Are you ready to set down the road to becoming a marketing manager? Let's see where you stand now.

Are you already working in marketing, advertising, public relations, or the like—or are you a manager? In many ways, the marketing manager job is merely a step up from jobs in these fields. In fact, you may just need to position for the responsibility of leadership to be ready.

Do you have relevant academic experience? Marketing is extremely influenced by the fields of economics, psychology, sociology, and, increasingly, anthropology. If you have academic experience in one of these fields, you are ahead of the game. Think of ways to spin your book knowledge so that it applies to marketing. A senior career changer may even be able to parlay a track record in one of these academic disciplines into an upper-level marketing manager post.

Do you really need to market yourself? Do not worry! Marketing can be highly industry-specific. Begin by looking for a job as a marketing manager in your original industry. Consider taking a bridge job to bolster your marketing-specific credentials while maintaining your industry connections. For instance, if you worked in the aerospace industry, you may want to look into marketing for a company that deals with the aerospace trade. Likewise, if you worked selling financial products for a bank,

Navigating the Terrain

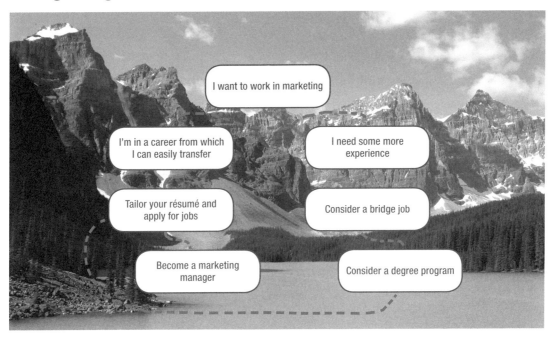

I want to work in marketing

I'm in a career from which I can easily transfer

I need some more experience

Tailor your résumé and apply for jobs

Consider a bridge job

Become a marketing manager

Consider a degree program

you may want to look at marketing IRAs, investment portfolios, and the like. You may also want to consider taking a second college degree, or perhaps a certificate program in marketing.

Organizing Your Expedition

Before you set out, know where you are going.

Decide on a destination. Obviously, you want to become a marketing manager. But how to get there? Follow the right path, and you will not go wrong.

Scout the terrain. What do companies in your industry look for in marketing managers? Investigate help-wanted ads and talk to people already working in the field. Be attuned to your environment: Observe different advertising approaches, note what trends change and what stay the same, and what techniques you find particularly effective.

Notes from the Field
Nicole C. Blackman
Marketing manager
New York, New York

What were you doing before you decided to change careers?

I was doing corporate philanthropy for financial services firms before deciding to change careers.

Why did you change your career?

I was tired of working in the financial services industry.

How did you make the transition?

While I love [corporate philanthropy], still some of the work was very similar to marketing-types of positions, so I transitioned my skills to a marketing position in a consumer-products company.

What are the keys to success in your new career?

I think the keys to success in my new career are to learn as much about the industry and my firm's competition, not be afraid to express new ideas or think out of the box, and try to learn as much as possible about the various areas of my company and help other teams on projects as much as possible.

Find the path that's right for you. What can you do to acquire the qualifications you lack? Do you need coursework? An MBA? A six-month transfer to the PR department? Whatever you need, make it happen.

Landmarks

If you are in your twenties . . . Career changers in the beginning of their working lives are optimally placed to become marketing managers. Your difficulty rests in your lack of experience, as the job is one that carries much responsibility. Put in the time to learn as much as you can working in marketing and PR departments, and you will be ready for a managerial opportunity when it presents itself.

If you are in your thirties or forties . . . Your seniority will be helpful in becoming a marketing manager. Your main problem may be that you have little experience in marketing. A bridge jobs in a related fields such as public relations, additional coursework—and careful tailoring of your résumé—can go a long way to overcoming these difficulties. Ask yourself what in your current job is similar to what a marketing manager does and capitalize on it when planning your move. Hone your research and math skills.

If you are in your fifties . . . Experienced employees are always in demand in upper-level positions. This is especially true if you can put your industry-specific skills, knowledge, and contacts to work for you. For instance, a professor of sociology might put his survey-conducting knowledge at the disposal of a marketing company. In more specific fields, such as trade marketing, the voice of experience is extremely respected.

If you are over sixty . . . Marketing manager is not a traditional second career, but that is not to say it is impossible. Much as for senior-level employees, you will want to play up your experience while minimizing the impression that you lag the times. Part of this is attitude and dress. Make sure you present an active, put-together appearance. Also make sure your résumé shows an unbroken history of productive employment, even if you have to fill in the gaps with freelance work or volunteering.

Further Resources

The Public Relations Society of America provides certification for Public Relations specialists. http://www.prsa.org

MarketingManager.com is a job listing and recruiting site for potential marketing managers. http://www.marketingmanager.com

Marketing Survey Researcher

Marketing Survey Researcher

Career Compasses

Here's the breakdown of what it takes to become a marketing survey researcher.

Relevant Knowledge of the methods and techniques of survey methods (30%)

Mathematical Skills especially in statistics (40%)

Organizational Skills to manage surveys (20%)

Communication Skills to report your findings (10%)

Destination: Marketing Survey Researcher

George Gallup's invention of modern methods of statistical sampling in the 1920s and 1930s was a watershed moment for both politics and marketing. Now, with a relatively small sample, the outcome of an election or a product's popularity could be accurately predicted. However, doing this accurately requires specialized mathematical skills and knowledge of both marketing and the science of statistics.

Marketing survey researchers are the specialists who can tell who wants to buy a product and how much they want to pay for it. They can determine a brand's "recognition" and predict future sales. To do so, they may conduct focus groups, make phone calls, send out questionnaires, or even go door-to-door. They must know both how to design and interpret surveys and how to explain the results to nonspecialists. All of this is critical to marketing success. In order to measure the public's response to a company's efforts, the results need to be quantified—as that old saying goes, "If you cannot measure it, you cannot manage it." Managers and policy makers therefore depend on marketing survey researchers' work in order to get maximum sales results and to make strategic decisions. Marketing survey researchers put into action the idea that the world can be quantitatively measured. They see modern marketing as a dynamic process in which both seller and consumer reach a middle ground on how, where, and for how much a product is sold.

Essential Gear

Primary versus secondary research. Primary research, in marketing jargon, is research one conducts oneself. Its advantage is that it is specific to the questions that need to be asked, but it is time-consuming and expensive. Secondary research is that which other people have compiled. The disadvantage is that it is often not wholly applicable to the problem at hand. However, it is quicker and cheaper to do.

Generally speaking, marketing survey researchers have specialized educations, with good computer skills and a concentration in math (particularly statistics and marketing survey courses) being prime factors. Computer skills are important because many marketing survey researchers use computers to input data and examine results. Also, computer graphics and presentation programs (such as Microsoft Office Suite programs Excel and PowerPoint) are how marketing survey researchers convey their findings to their audiences. Other coursework may be in psychology, communications, and marketing. These are essential both to understand the principles of marketing and to effectively design surveys. Though most marketing survey researchers have at least a bachelor's degree in this field or a closely related one, master's degrees and Ph.D.s are even more sought after. It is also necessary to keep abreast of the latest research and techniques. You will need to attend conferences and subscribe to trade journals in order to keep current with the latest tools.

Marketing survey researchers are much in demand in the worlds of both advertising and politics, and many transition between the two. One can easily understand the similarities. Much as advertising companies want to know what the public thinks, so too do politicians. How popular are their policies? What is the public reaction to the candidate's the latest speech? Who is going to likely win the election? What elements of policy does the public agree with? All of these are critical questions to which policy makers require definite answers.

The theory of marketing survey research is that a randomly selected group of people from a given population will represent a microcosm of that population. If 70 people out of 100 have heard of Brand A, then you should expect, on average, that 7 out of 10 people randomly selected from that population to have heard of Brand A—plus or minus a certain percentage of error. The trick is selecting these people. You might set up a polling place in a shopping mall—but suppose for a moment that Brand A appeals to the sorts of people who do not visit malls. In this case, you might get a biased survey and find that less people have heard of Brand A than actually have. You might call people at home, but people who generally like Brand A may have themselves placed on the do-not-call list. Mail surveys tend to have low responses, and Internet surveys tend to exclude those without online access. One easily gets an idea of the difficulties that a pollster encounters.

Surveys can take two basic forms. One is the *self-administered survey,* that is, a questionnaire. The other is the *researcher-administered survey,* or the *structured interview.* Researcher-administered surveys tend to have higher response rates and a better understanding of the questions for the respondents, but they are time-consuming. Surveys can also be *serial,* that is, given more than once so that researchers can see change over time. The two types of serial surveys are *cross-sectional and longitudinal.* A cross-sectional survey uses a new sample of the population each time it is given, while a longitudinal survey surveys the same sample more than once. Surveys are usually standardized (that is, everyone gets the same questions in the same order) so that the results are reliable and can be compared with one another. Survey construction is another sensitive topic. The survey itself must be carefully constructed so that the answers to later questions are not biased by previous questions.

Surveys are an excellent way of easily and reliably collecting large amounts of different types of information. For all of this, surveys can be flawed. The collection of factual information relies on participants' cooperation, memory, need to be seen as good people, and desire to respond honestly. Many surveys use closed-ended questions that reflect the researchers' bias, or do not give a true sense of possible responses. If there are only boxes for "yes" and "no," then "maybe" is not an option. Alternatively, the presented choices can be *too vague*. Also, there is always a level of error due to statistical bias or non-response to questions.

A marketing survey research campaign will progress through several basic steps. The first is to *define the problem*. What are you trying to measure? What information do you need? How will the necessary concepts be defined, and how are these translated into measurable data? Is there a hypothesis you can state that can be tested? This is the stage that requires the most abstract thought, but in turn it will guide your *research design*. This is the stage in which you decide what sort of methodology to use, such as a questionnaire or a personal survey, as well as *question specification* (what the questions will be and what order they will appear in), *scale*

Essential Gear

Political campaign research. Everyone is familiar with the "talking heads" on TV pulling out seemingly incontrovertible statistics on the latest political campaign. But where do these numbers come from? While the goals of political survey analysis are very different from market surveying, the methods are similar. Political pollsters take surveys of random samplings of voters, whether by telephone interviewing, stopping them on the street or at the polling place, or by any other method. They ask the voters which candidate they favor, as well as how they feel about various issues. Finally, they record information about the voters themselves—age, race, education level, and socioeconomic status being the prime examples. Candidates use the data to see what people in various groups think about them, find out what their concerns are, and to modify their campaign strategy accordingly. While this may all seem cynical, it is in fact an important tool of democracy. It allows potential elected officials to realize what the people *really* want to see—in other words, it lets the broader constituency affect policy.

specification (the format in which you will be collecting answers, such as "Yes or No" or on a 1 to 10 variable scale), and the *sampling design*, in which you determine what sort of sample size you will need to get an idea of the overall population. The methodology used will often depend on other variables, such as what you are trying to measure, the sample size you need, and what sort of questions you are asking.

The next step is to actually collect the data, using some of the methods listed above—direct mail, telephone, Internet, polling in public places, or going door-to-door. After the raw data is collected, it is standardized so that it can be analyzed using traditional statistical techniques. Only then can the data be interpreted, conclusions drawn from the results, and the hypothesis verified, rejected, or modified. The whole effort, which may take months (or even years for a major strategy shift), is then distilled into a research report (preferably with easy-to-understand charts and diagrams) than can be delivered in ten minutes.

Marketing survey researchers' hours tend to be regular, though overtime is not uncommon when facing a deadline or on a tight election campaign. About 261,000 market and survey researchers were employed in the United States as of 2006, according to the U.S. Bureau of Labor Statistics. They can be found in all sectors of the advertising industry, from big Madison Avenue firms to small local concerns, as well as working within industries themselves (that is, directly employed by the companies that produce goods and services for various markets). A marketing survey researcher who works for a bank, for instance, might learn about the bank's clientele's needs to ensure they are being met. The financial compensation for the job can vary. Marketing survey researchers earn a median of $58,820, with the lowest 10 percent earning less than $32,250 and the highest 10 percent earning over $112,510, according to 2006 figures from the U.S. Bureau of Labor Statistics. Those with specialized expertise in computer systems—an invaluable tool of the modern marketing survey researcher—tended to be the highest-earners.

Those who are experienced and have previous education in math, statistics, and demography are the best placed to transition into careers as marketing survey researchers. Nonetheless, while a certain amount of learning is on-the-job, additional education is often necessary. You may need to go back to school to earn a degree such as a master of survey research (MSR). Such coursework is usually full-time and intensive, leaving little opportunity to learn outside of class. Expect to devote yourself to school for at least a year. Those in such programs will learn the latest polling and interpretation methods, (as well as the limitations of such techniques), and how to communicate the results to a lay audience.

You Are Here

Are you ready to set down the road to becoming a marketing survey researcher? Let's see where you stand now.

Do you have a background in demographics, sociology, or another related discipline? Your mathematical and statistical skills are invaluable. However, you might still need additional training, since marketing survey researchers have a very specialized toolset. The Marketing Research Association (MRA) also offers a certification program. You may also need experience before going on the job market. Consider taking an internship, volunteering for an organization that requires your skills, or working on a political campaign.

Do you come from another background? Because of the specific nature of the marketing survey researcher job, you will probably need to go back to school. Marketing survey researchers need to know psychology, statistics, and polling strategies, among other skills. This is a math-heavy course load. Be sure to brush up on your mathematic skills, especially calculus.

Investigate degree programs in your area. How much will they cost? How long will they take? Is financial aid available? Will previous coursework transfer? How will you pay your rent or mortgage while you are in school? Who will take care of your children? Will your family support your decision? Online learning, in whole or in part, is another possibility.

Organizing Your Expedition

Before you set out, know where you are going.

Decide on a destination. Becoming a marketing survey researcher is a very specific career path. The essential question is how much additional training you will need to retool yourself for the journey.

Scout the terrain. Look at help-wanted ads, search the Web (especially the MRA's Web site (see "Further Resources") and make contact with

Navigating the Terrain

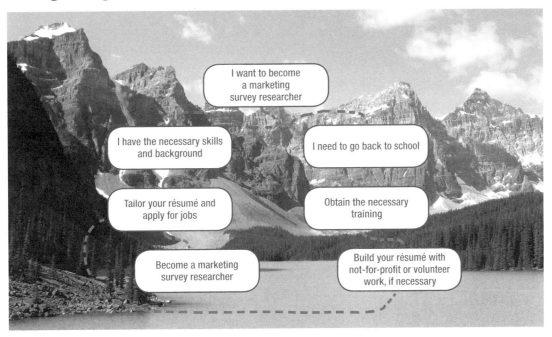

I want to become
a marketing
survey researcher

I have the necessary skills
and background

I need to go back to school

Tailor your résumé and
apply for jobs

Obtain the necessary
training

Become a marketing
survey researcher

Build your résumé with
not-for-profit or volunteer
work, if necessary

people working in the field. Do you have enough expertise to learn on the job? Or do you need other qualifications?

Find the path that's right for you. Schooling is not the only thing you need for this new career: Experience is also essential. Look for volunteer opportunities and political campaigns you can work on. Another possibility is internships. Often, this goes hand-in-hand with a degree program, since organizations often mine local universities for help.

Landmarks

If you are in your twenties . . . Workers in their twenties, especially those with a background in statistical and numerical professions, are in prime positions to go back to school and retool as marketing survey researchers. It may help to join an organization such as the MRA to make valuable contacts and learn tips from seasoned veterans.

Notes from the Field
Samuel Webb
Marketing survey researcher
New York, New York

What were you doing before you decided to change careers?

I was working in the accounting department in a now-defunct Web site design company in New York and San Francisco. Over the three-plus years that I worked for this company across different accounting functions I processed A/R, A/P, deferrals, leases, billing allocations, and various other accounting functions.

Why did you change your career?

I was not happy working in accounting, and I wanted to do something more meaningful than just dollars and cents, so I started in the direction of politics/government. It seemed to be more interesting than balance sheets. I found market research by accident, or perhaps I was just destined to find another type of number crunching that worked better with my personality.

How did you make the transition?

The transition was not short by any means. Initially I decided I wanted to go to school for government. I got into the University of Connecticut master of public administration program (two days before my entire office was laid off). During my first year I found the master of survey research (MSR) program at UConn, which was part of the same department (at the time I did not even know market research existed as a discipline). We shared some classes with those students, and I became intrigued with market research and public opinion. After much consideration I transferred into the MSR Program and never looked back.

However, upon graduation from the MSR program I was having difficulty finding a job with the firms that I wanted to work at. Oftentimes I could not even get an interview for the most entry-level of jobs. So in consultation with friends and acquaintances in politics I determined that I needed to join a campaign to earn some political experience.

I joined the field staff of a major presidential primary campaign in New Hampshire. (Luckily for me the campaign that I joined won the nomination.) I opted not to take a reassignment to the general election campaign because I was more interested in moving into public opinion research. The long hours and exposure to how political campaigns operate came in handy in landing my first professional market research job at a political and corporate market research firm.

The combination of my degree and political work were highlighted as the two key components in why this firm hired me. However, I know that the political campaign made a big difference. I had applied to this firm a half a dozen times before joining the campaign, and after the campaign I sent them a résumé and had an interview 15 minutes after hitting the send button (and I was hired one week later to work in DC). The only difference in my résumé [was] the campaign. The "gamble" worked.

I have slowly been moving away from political work for various reasons: 1) the hours are longer; 2) the pay is less; 3) the career path is slower; 4) the stress level is higher; and most importantly 5) I realized it was market research not politics that I wanted to make my life's work. Now I work in the custom market research department at a major business and news publication in New York. This combines all of my careers skills in business, politics, and market research. It is the best of all worlds.

What are the keys to success in your new career?

The keys to success are simple:

a)   *Attention to detail*

b)   *Hard work and dedication*

c)   *Show up everyday and do the best that you can*

d)   *Be willing to take risks*

e)   *Devise a plan and follow it*

f)   *When in doubt, fake it until you make it (but do not forget to ask questions)*

If you are in your thirties or forties . . . Mid-career workers might have more difficulty transitioning to this career. It becomes more important to begin from a point as closely related as possible to the work that a marketing survey researcher does. If, however, you are not current with the field, you will also probably need to go back to school.

If you are in your fifties . . . At this point in your career, it is often difficult to retool. However, the world of market survey research may not be closed to you if you can bring something unique and valuable to the table. For instance, a professor of statistics or sociology might find him- or herself a niche in the profession.

If you are over sixty . . . At this age, returning to school might not be the best idea. However, second-career starters with contacts and expertise who see an opportunity in their areas might want to consider founding their own market research survey companies. You may be able to find clients through your old business network and through people in your community. You can also volunteer your services to local political candidates, who will be glad for the help and probably recommend your services as well.

Further Resources

The Council of American Survey Research Organizations (CASRO) is the industry organization for this profession, concentrating on advocacy and also standards and ethics of research. http://www.casro.org
The Marketing Research Association (MRA) is the professional organization for marketing survey researchers. http://www.mra-net.org

Trade Show Representative or Coordinator

Trade Show Representative or Coordinator

Career Compasses

Here's the breakdown of what it takes to become a trade show representative or coordinator.

Relevant Knowledge of your product and the industry (30%)

Caring—that is, people skills (10%)

Organizational Skills to put everything together (30%)

Communication Skills to sell, sell, sell (30%)

Destination: Trade Show Representative or Coordinator

Trade shows are exhibitions organized to showcase products and services in a particular industry. This is a very old tradition, going back possibly to the medieval textile industry's renowned Champagne trade fairs that brought merchants to northern France from all over Europe. Wool merchants from England, dyers from Italy, and weavers from Flanders used to meet here and discuss prices. The Champagne fairs enabled the international commerce of the day to take place.

Today, trade shows remain must-attend events for people working in many industries. Some trade shows are open to the public, while others are industry- and press-only. Many modern trade shows, like the video game industry's E3 Media and Business Summit (formerly known as Electronic Entertainment Expo) are exciting, fun affairs that have become virtual pilgrimages for the industry's faithful devotees. Their presence has become so overwhelming in recent years, with attendances swelling to 70,000 people, that E3 was forced to become an invitation-only event in 2007. E3 remains heavily featured by both the mainstream press and publications that cover the video gaming industry exclusively, and invitations are highly coveted. Passes to the event are valued as if they were tickets to a rock concert.

Other trade shows that similarly hold a broad interest for a large group of people, such as those dealing with cars (such as auto shows), publishing (such as the famed Frankfurt Book Fair), or horses (where vendors of tack, fencing, and other supplies might exhibit their wares), hold mass appeal. There are lots of other types of trade shows, such as those devoted to life insurance or building trades, that have narrower appeal but are no less necessary to the companies that rely on them to create awareness of their products. They provide opportunities to display their products to the industry and/or the public; to interact and network with potential business partners, suppliers, and clients; to make sales; to garner press coverage; and to get feedback on their products. Most companies consider the rewards reaped in publicity and networking—as well as the opportunity to keep an eye on the competitors—to be well worth the outlay of cash.

What all of these types of shows have in common is their need for experienced trade show representatives and coordinators. Trade show representatives are the professionals who attend trade shows on behalf of a company, represent its products and interests, keep an eye on competitors, and do the networking with potential vendors and clients. They are in charge of handling space rental; designing and constructing the displays; making sure that company representatives have access to wireless Internet, telephones, fax machines, and other telecommunications necessities; arranging for travel and accommodations; and overseeing the design of promotional materials. Trade show representatives or coordinators may also work for the trade shows themselves, trying to convince companies to exhibit and helping to set up the exhibitions. Some work in a freelance capacity with either (or both) of the two sides.

Essential Gear

Types of trade show displays. There are several different types of trade show displays, ranging from the very simple to the very complicated. Being versed in what is available will help you on your way to becoming a trade show representative.

The most basic form of display is the *pipe and drape*. This is sometimes provided with the exhibit space. It is a pipe frame set into base plates to which a fabric drape is attached via ties or a sewn-in sleeve. They are very basic, but can provide a backdrop and sometimes enough support to attach graphics.

Tabletop displays are simply printed tablecloths for the tables in your booth. They are easy for one person to set up, but not very dynamic. One step up from this is a *pull-up display*, which has a scrolling graphic panel that one person can operate. This is very light, but also slightly fragile.

A *modular exhibit* or *custom exhibit* gets fancier. *Modular* exhibits either make use of existing structures (like the pipes and drapes) or are made to be easy to transport and assemble. They offer a great deal of flexibility in delivering your sales pitch, whether it is graphics or a simple prop. *Custom* exhibits can be anything you like, from a model of a car engine to a castle made of Styrofoam bricks to a complicated audiovisual display. While they may leave room for your creativity, it is important not to be tempted to make them too large or unwieldy. In this case, you may need to contact the trade show's approved labor force in order to put them together.

Trade show displays refer to a company's physical presence at the show. Their design and construction is an end in itself. Generally, they are intended to represent a single idea and feature bright, bold, colorful images and slogans. They may have audiovisual displays, diagrams, samples of the product, models, and other experiential attractions. However, they must also fit the constraints of the medium. The usual trade-show booth in the United States is 10 feet by 10 feet; in the rest of the world it is usually three meters by three meters, with additional space available in increments of one square meter. Some trade show displays are permanent and re-used year after year; others are "build and burn" and disposed of after a single show. The sort you use will depend both on budget constraints and the nature of the show.

An important distinction in the type of trade shows you might attend is a *horizontal* versus a *vertical* market. Vertical shows tend to be narrowly focused for one type of market, such as chiropractors or MRI machine manufacturers. Horizontal shows tend to be on subjects of broad interest that affect a number of industries. An example is occupational safety or superconductors. Whereas chiropractors' tables and MRI machines are not of much interest to people who are not chiropractors or hospital administrators, many industries have a vested interest in preventing workplace accidents, and superconductors are used in a wide range of medical, engineering, and scientific applications. Of course, horizontality or verticality is no measure of a trade show's potential draw. E3 and Entertainment for All are about as vertical as you can get (being exclusively video-game oriented), but still get massive crowds.

Running a trade show, whether as an exhibitor or a host, requires great layouts of money. Because they bring in so many people and so much money, cities often promote themselves as ideal trade show locations. Local governments may offer financial incentives to draw business. Trade shows are important to cities not only for showing status but also for contributing to economic activity by providing jobs and selling goods. Due to the lucrative contracts and possibilities for profit, there are often strict regulations on who can be hired for what. For instance, there may be a rule stating that any heavy lifting and carting must be performed by union members. A good trade show representative or coordinator keeps well-appraised of all of these regulations, and knows how to work with them.

Another problem that a trade show representative might run into, especially when traveling abroad, are airlines and customs regulations. Airlines limit how much baggage you may carry and have related fees for carrying oversize or excess luggage can be costly. In some cases, it may be financially advantageous to ship your samples or displays ahead of you—in which case you will also have to arrange for pick-up and storage. Customs officials may consider product samples for soliciting orders as merchandise, and you may need to declare and pay a duty on them. A good trade show representative also knows how to work with and around the various travel limitations.

One downside of trade shows is the aforementioned expense. Thus, with the rising costs of everything, trade shows are increasingly being held online. "Virtual tradeshows" are similar to brick-and-mortar tradeshows, complete with an "exhibitor's hall" and "booths," except that they are held in cyberspace and staffed via telecommunications. Instead of sitting in the booth, the trade show representative waits behind his or her computer terminal to make contacts and answer questions. Thus it is possible to meet with like-minded people and establish business contacts without leaving one's chair (although the quality of networking is not so rich as with live shows). As this segment of the industry grows, it is likely that trade show representatives will need to become increasingly computer-savvy. A downside of this sort of trade show is that, while multimedia displays can be very snazzy, it is difficult to get a good idea of what something looks like, or get the feel for someone's personality, in cyberspace.

While you do not need too much formal education or experience to become a trade show representative (though a marketing degree is helpful and the Convention Industry Council offers Meeting Professional certification), this is a career path with a definite bias toward attractive, outgoing, charismatic people. Those who plan such events must naturally have a flair for organization and coordination. Trade shows have a lot of paperwork to fill out, and things must be kept to a tight timetable. It helps to have strong social networks in the applicable industry (or at least have an ability to develop them), and to be a persuasive seller. Not only do you need to sell your clients' products to potential customers, but, from the other end, you must convince potential clients and exhibitors that the trade show is worth their investment of money and time. Finally, strong communication skills in order to come up with promotional materials and explain why your product is the best are a necessity.

The hours of a trade show representative or coordinator are often long and may include a good deal of travel, both domestic and international. However, the rewards are rich. While some people might consider trade show planning and representing to be stressful, most find work in the field energizing and exciting. The rewards are also financial. According to the U.S. Bureau of Labor Statistics, about 51,000 convention and meeting planners were employed in the United States in 2006 and made a median salary of $42,180. The best paid tended to work in private industry. Product demonstrators (which includes trade show representatives) held about 118,000 jobs in the United States and made a median income of $9.95 per hour. If you want to transfer to become a convention and meeting planner, it is best—though not strictly necessary—to have a background in marketing. Of course, what is even more important is to have sound communication, organizational, and interpersonal skills, and a good measure of charisma.

You Are Here

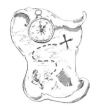

Do you want to enter the exciting world of trade shows? You can approach your goal from several directions.

Do you have a background in sales, marketing, or public relations? Very good! You probably already have a lot of the skills you need, and your résumé is ready to be re-shaped to fit a new career as a trade show representative or coordinator. Emphasize your planning and management experience, and do not be afraid to take a bridge job to fill in any gaps in your knowledge.

Are you experienced at working with the public? Charisma is paramount in this occupation. While some universities do offer degrees in meeting management, most learning takes place on the job. Look for an entry-level position that will enable you to take on more responsibility as you gain more experience. In the enthusiasm department, it is all but essential that you actually like the product.

Do you come from another field? Again, not to worry. Every industry has its own trade shows. Find out what the big ones are in your field of expertise and see what opportunities are available. You may want to enhance your résumé, whether through formal education, an internship, or a bridge job. Perhaps the best example of a possible bridge job to becoming a trade show representative or coordinator is working as a sales representative. Company sales representatives are often given the task of attending trade shows, setting up booths, and finding staffing. This can be a good opportunity for you to see how such events are run, as well as to make valuable contacts. In this case, practical, hands-on experience is probably a much better teacher than any other path to this career goal.

Navigating the Terrain

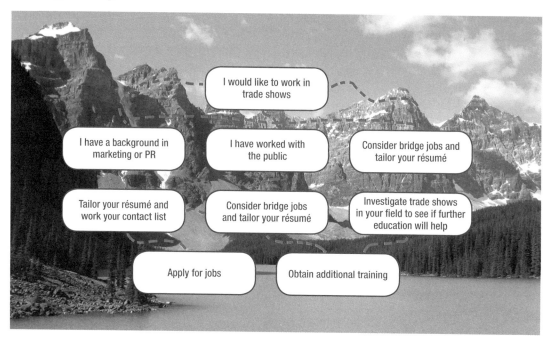

I would like to work in trade shows

I have a background in marketing or PR

I have worked with the public

Consider bridge jobs and tailor your résumé

Tailor your résumé and work your contact list

Consider bridge jobs and tailor your résumé

Investigate trade shows in your field to see if further education will help

Apply for jobs

Obtain additional training

Organizing Your Expedition

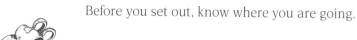

Before you set out, know where you are going.

Decide on a destination. The path you take to becoming a trade show representative or coordinator is up to you. It depends on your background and training.

Scout the terrain. First, determine how qualified you are for the job. Do you have experience in a particular industry? Have you ever worked a trade show before? Do you have management experience? Public relations? Marketing? Look at what companies advertising open positions are looking for.

Find the path that's right for you. Tailor your résumé to emphasize your experience and qualifications. Naturally, the more similar your past experience has been to being a trade show representative, the easier things will be. Nevertheless, trade show representative or coordinator can be

Notes from the Field
Jim Fulmer
Trade show representative
Chicago, Illinois

What were you doing before you decided to change careers?

I had a business rebuilding and also selling grand pianos.

Why did you change your career?

Unfortunately, the labor costs in rebuilding pianos are prohibitive, and no one plays, much less wants to have a piano rebuilt, any more. When I closed my shop, I reversed the ratio of rebuilding/service to sales in my business—90 percent rebuilding to 10 percent sales changed to 90 percent sales and 10 percent service.

How did you make the transition?

I became a sales representative for a piano company. Like many sales representatives, attending trade shows is part of my job. I'd already had experience doing trade shows for my wife's tile-making business, so when I switched jobs, it was an easy enough transition.

What are the keys to success in your new career?

It is pretty easy. One stands around in the booth grinning, talking, attempting to get passersby to step up and consider the merchandise. I'd say the most important thing in this aspect of the job is that you have to be personable.

an easy job to transition into if you have the right inclination and talents—and, of course, a bridge job or additional college coursework never hurts. Also look into the Convention Industry Council's Certified Meeting Professional certification. (See their Web site in "Further Resources.")

Landmarks

If you are in your twenties . . . Your chances of changing careers are excellent, especially if you are interested in doing trade shows for industries that market toward a younger, hipper crowd. If you need to, consider going back to school or taking a bridge job to transition to this career path.

If you are in your thirties or forties . . . Put your specialized knowledge and previous experience to work for you. Your time spent learning an industry's ins and outs means that you can do wonders for a company at vertically-organized trade shows. Be sure to emphasize your previous experience.

If you are in your fifties . . . While senior-level employees are often at a disadvantage in changing to public appearance-oriented careers, you are still in a strong position to use your connections and knowledge to start your own business as a trade show representative or coordinator.

If you are over sixty . . . Respected senior-level or second-career employees can do wonders in the trade-show world. As the voice of experience, you are can speak authoritatively of a product's virtues. You are also in a position to mine your wealth of contacts.

Further Resources

How Trade Shows Work A useful explanation from HowStuffWorks.com. http://money.howstuffworks.com/trade-show.htm
Professional Convention Management Association Everything you have ever wanted to know about managing conventions. http://www.pcma.org
Meeting Professionals International The trade organization for the meeting industry. Includes a career guide. http://www.mpiweb.org/cms/mpiweb/default.aspx
The Convention Industry Council Offers the Certified Meeting Professional credential. http://www.conventionindustry.org

Copywriter

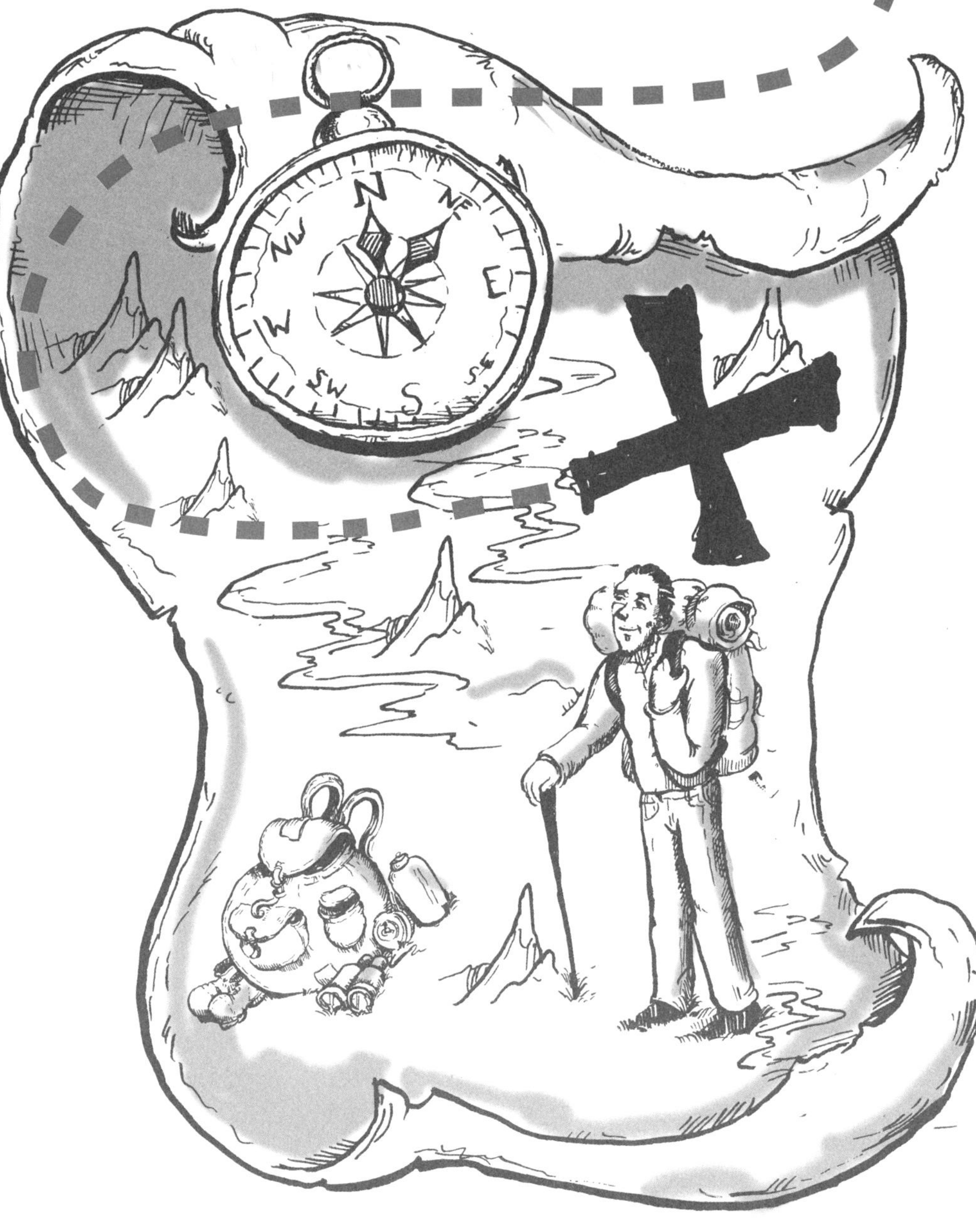

Copywriter

Career Compasses

Here's the breakdown of what it takes to become a copywriter.

Relevant Knowledge of what you are selling. You have to know the facts before you can communicate them to an audience (20%)

Caring about what you are writing about makes the difference between good copy and hammering out filler (20%)

Organizational Skills to stay on deadline are very important (20%)

Communication Skills to come up with witty taglines and spellbinding prose are, of course, the prime requisite! (40%)

Destination: Copywriter

"Keeps going and going." "Where's the beef?" "Is it live, or is it Memorex?" If you can name the products and brands associated with these advertising slogans, thank (or blame) copywriters, the talented individuals who dream up the words and ideas that sell the products of our everyday lives. While copywriting is related to technical writing, its intent is primarily to persuade, not to inform, the consumer. (Although, of course, information can be a form of persuasion.) At their best, copywriters can come up with the jingles, slogans, and phrases that define a generation. If you are of a certain age, the slogans quoted in the first sentence recalled not only products, but entire epochs of modern life. At its worst, copywriting can be sheer drudgery. Nonetheless, it remains one of the most-desired careers in advertising. Copywriters are not only rewarded with high pay and high status within their profession; they can also rise to the top of the ad-world hierarchy.

Along with the art directors, designers, and other visual workers with whom they work closely, copywriters are half of the creative engine that moves the advertising world. Their job includes not just coming up with brief, catchy slogans, but also pamphlets, jingles, direct mailings, and even book-length projects. Some copywriters' jobs shade more into that of screenwriter, in that they create scripts for radio and television ads. Such copywriters must have an ear for language as it is spoken, for drama, and for visual thinking—and must keep the message within the 30-second or one-minute timeframe. The fruits of copywriters' labor are incorporated into overall marketing, publicity, and public relations plans. They must be well-informed about the advertising campaign's overall game plan. What is the overall message? What attitude is sought? What group is trying to be reached? Reading the promotional plan is essential, as is good communication between all branches of the advertising staff. While everyone is looking for the next creative genius, those who are not team players tend to be less appreciated.

Some copywriting projects are limited only by the writers' creativity, while others may be more tightly constrained. Pharmaceutical ads, for instance, must by law include both benefits and side effects of the advertised medication. Another example is the "small print" in ads for everything from cell phone plans to automobiles that must be included in order to adhere to truth-in-advertising regulations. Space is also a consideration. There may be only so much space in a direct mailer, or so many characters that can fit "above the fold" (that is, the part you can initially see upon loading) on a Web page. This is one reason why it is important to coordinate closely with your design team.

Of course, copywriting is not all about dreaming up scintillating text. It also involves a lot of proofreading and copyediting. Thus, being a good editor and having an ear for language are also basic skills. Attention to detail is important, particularly in fields such as pharmaceuticals where precision is mandatory. Even in less strictly regulated industries, typos and errors can be embarrassing. As an advertising copywriter, you will be spending a lot of time going over your—and others'—text. This part of the job can be very stressful. advertising copywriters work under strict deadlines. You may not always be "into" what you are selling, and there may be times when you feel like you simply cannot wax rhapsodic about savings accounts or dietary supplements any longer. Nonetheless, the work is mostly creative and stimulating, and the possibilities for advancement are many. Though not as high-earning as some other careers in advertising, advertising copywriters are still well-paid. According to the U.S. Bureau of Labor Statistics, writers and editors who worked in the advertising industry earned a median salary of $50,650 in 2006.

While most advertising copywriters work in firms owned by other people, some are freelancers and others even own their own businesses. According to the U.S. Bureau of Labor Statistics, about 458,000 of all advertising workers were salary workers in 2006, whereas 46,800 were self-employed. Though many live in California and New York, advertising copywriters can be found throughout the nation.

Essential Gear

In addition to television and radio ads, here are some of the things you might find yourself writing as an advertising copywriter:

Direct mail: Familiar to anyone with a mailbox, this a campaign of promotional materials mailed out directly to consumers. This is also sometimes referred to as "long copy" in the industry.

Body copy: As opposed to headlines, slogans, and jingles, this is the block of substantial text that gives information and seeks to persuade consumers about the product or service.

Press release: An announcement given to media sources proclaiming something "newsworthy," such as a product release.

White paper: When used in a commercial context, a document that sets forth the benefits of a particular product or service. Generally, a white paper will try to persuade consumers why a company's products are best.

Most work in small businesses instead of the huge Madison Avenue "shops." In a small business, roles can be less stringently defined. One might wear many hats besides that of copywriter. You may find yourself compelled to contribute to the design team, or be given management responsibilities as creative director. Many people find that they enjoy doing the "fill-in" job better than what they were hired to do, or are actually better at it! This is one way to change careers within the advertising industry, but it is not a good idea to count on it.

There are not many pure copywriters working in advertising today. Only about 8,000 people, or 1.8 percent of the industry, claimed to be "writers or authors" in 2006. The number of job applicants usually vastly exceeds the number of available positions. However, the sector is expanding. The World Wide Web has opened up numerous new opportunities for advertising copywriters. Some new media copywriters engage in guerilla marketing by creating blogs, posting on message boards, and generally using new media to try to get the word out about the products they have been hired to promote.

There is no set path to become an advertising copywriter. One not-uncommon career trajectory is for and advertising copywriter is to major in English, communications, or another similar subject and then take an entry-level job in the industry. However, this is not the only way one may begin. What is valued most of all is sheer creativity and the willingness to put it to use. It is no coincidence that many creative individuals such as Terry Gilliam of Monty Python and the writer Salman Rushdie worked as copywriters.

Perhaps the single most useful thing you can do to aid your job search is to create a portfolio. This need not be work you have been hired to do, though showing that people will pay for your services is always a help. Rather, try coming up with mock ads or ad scripts for either real or imaginary (but plausibly generic) products. For this, it is not enough just to have the copy—you should have actual samples of full-production, full-color sample ad in a variety of formats, whether for magazines or billboards, to show prospective employers.

To get started, you will need access to a variety of things. The first and most important is a trove of arresting images to go with your copy. If you do not know any photographers, stock photos from agencies such as Corbis (http://www.corbis.com) can be invaluable assets. Sites like these will allow you to search through their enormous banks of images and, for a fee, download files large enough to be used in print media. The second step is creating a good layout and design. Find a friend or associate who has knowledge of graphic design, or learn these skills yourself and acquire the necessary software (excellent books on art direction abound—check with local libraries or search for used copies on

Amazon.com). Make sure you mirror the conventions and format of the ads you are trying to replicate. Set up your text and images, and be sure to get feedback from impartial judges on how everything looks. And be sure to thoroughly proofread your work! The finished product can be presented in hard copy (make sure to keep copies for yourself) or in digital format. In fact, uploading a digital portfolio to your own Web site is an excellent way to make contacts and for potential bosses or clients to see what you can do. Besides sending along links with your job applications, you can also get the word out by participating on Web discussion boards frequented by those in the industry. If you do a good job, this nontraditional approach might just land you a job in advertising!

You Are Here

Want to earn a living with your pen? Take stock of where you are.

Do you have a background in sales, marketing, or public relations? Many copywriters have background in other areas of interest related to the advertising industry. However, these are not necessarily the keys that will unlock the door. Creativity, not book knowledge, is paramount. Be sure to emphasize your creative side and your writing experience in applying for jobs.

Are you a professional working in a creative industry? Those working in creative fields, such as film and music, have a good background for becoming advertising copywriters. Creativity itself is seen as *prima facie* evidence of having "the right stuff." This goes doubly for those working with words, or, even better, words and images together. Herschell Gordon Lewis, for instance, went from being a producer and director of B-movies to a successful advertising career.

Are you a making a cold pitch? Again, remember that creativity is the number-one requirement for this job. The most important thing in your job application is going to be a history of creative work. Take on freelance assignments, get short stories and articles published: in short, build a portfolio as a creative professional. You might also want to consider freelancing to build up a résumé.

Navigating the Terrain

I want to go into copywriting

Emphasize your creative side

Get bridge jobs writing copy and build a portfolio

Tailor your résumé

Apply for jobs

Organizing your Expedition

Before you set out, know where you are going.

Decide on a destination. So, you would like to become an advertising copywriter. Look at help-wanted ads, particularly on Web sites such as the *New York Times* (http://www.nytimes.com) that carry a lot of advertising agencies' ads. What are these firms asking for? What sorts of qualifications do their current employees have?

Scout the terrain. Having researched what employers are looking for, what can you do to make yourself more appealing to the people doing the hiring? While an MFA in creative writing will not necessarily help, a history of creative work and a proven ability to come up with winning copy on demand will. The question, then, is how to tailor your résumé to show that you have these abilities.

Stories from the Field
William Bernbach
Advertising pioneer—square among the hip

A little girl stands in a field, pulling the petals off a daisy. "One. two. three. four. five. seven," she counts. Suddenly, a terrifying military accent echoes its own countdown in the viewer's ears: "Ten. nine. eight. seven." A mushroom cloud fills the screen, annihilating the little girl and her field of flowers. "Vote for President Johnson on November 3," says the announcer. "The stakes are too high for you to stay home."

Lyndon Johnson's 1964 "Daisy" ad may be the most controversial advertisement of all time. It also may have won him the election. It, along with many other iconic ads of the 1960s, was the brainchild of William Bernbach, the copywriter-cum-advertising pioneer. Known for his own conservative suit-and-tie demeanor, Bernbach at the same time surrounded himself with creative types and had a fondness for unusual and offbeat ideas that grabbed the consumer's attention—classic campaigns such as the counterintuitive and brilliant Volkswagen "Think Small" campaign that, by showing a tiny, so-ugly-its-cute Beetle in one corner of a field of white space, not only challenged American ideas of what an automobile should be, but also introduced the first successful import car to the United States. It was ideas like this, as well as his combining copywriters and art directors into two-person teams, that made Bernbach one of the driving influences of advertising's so-called "Creative Revolution" of the 1960s and 1970s. As he himself said, "Rules are what the artist breaks; the memorable never emerged from a formula."

Bernbach credited much of his success to the fact that he did not begin in advertising. As he once said in an interview, "[By] not

Find the path that's right for you. The thing to do now is to gain the necessary experience to transfer your skills and abilities to become an advertising copywriter. Look for opportunities to build your résumé. Donate or volunteer your time to local political campaigns and not-for-profits; come up with slogans for local businesses; take on freelance work; and find a bridge job that gives you an in to the world of writing for a living. One important point: remember that copyediting is one small step from copywriting.

knowing too much about advertising. I could be fresher and more original about it. As soon as you become a slave to the rules, you're doing what everybody else does; when you do what everybody else does, you do not stand out." Born in 1911, Bernbach grew up in the Bronx and graduated from New York University in 1932. The Depression was in full swing, and he was lucky to find a mailroom job at Schenley Distillers. It was at Schenley that he made the acquaintance of Grover Whalen, the company chairman and a well-connected official in the New York business world. When Whalen left the company to direct the 1939 World's Fair, Bernbach left with him and became a staff writer. He used this as a bridge job to become a copywriter in 1941 at the William Weintraub agency. It was his close relationship with legendary art director Paul Rand at Weintraub that led him to theorize about the complementary relationship between design and copy.

During his time at Weintraub, and at Grey Advertising from 1945 to 1949, and finally at Doyle Dane Bernbach—his own firm which he led until his death of leukemia in 1982—Bill Bernbach achieved legendary success. His agency achieved over a billion dollars in billings, changing the field of advertising and the entire American cultural landscape in the process. Bernbach left the actual running of the agency to his partners, preferring to keep on the creative side of things—albeit only representing those products that he felt were worthy of great advertising. "Nothing makes a bad product fail faster than a great advertising campaign" is the saying that he is perhaps most remembered for. However, an equally fitting epitaph might be another Bernbach quote: "All of us who professionally use the mass media are the shapers of society. We can vulgarize that society. We can brutalize it. Or we can help lift it onto a higher level."

Landmarks

If you are in your twenties . . . Early-career changers, particularly those with experience in writing, are in a good position to become advertising copywriters. Still, there is much you can do to boost your résumé. Take on freelance work or volunteer your time to gain experience. You may also want to look at an internship or bridge job. Remember that most advertising copywriters do not do very exciting work at first: they often begin editing or proofreading other peoples' writing or drafting long lists of disclaimers for pharmaceutical companies. Your youth and perceived hipness can work for you, but at the same time make sure to appear responsible and serious-minded.

If you are in your thirties or forties . . . Mid-career changers with a history of creative work are in the best position to change to advertising copywriting. The level you enter at will be a function of your experience. You may be able to "jump over" the entry-level positions that twenty-somethings land in. Nevertheless, much of the same advice applies to you. Build your résumé with freelance work and volunteering. You will be in the best position to change if you are a published author or have done other writing for pay. Remember that advertising is often youth-centered. If you made it through young adulthood without being hip, now is the time to get with the program; in the quasi-creative professions, uncoolness is penalized in direct proportion to how old you are. But one caveat—the cardinal sin is to try too hard.

Essential Gear

Search engine optimization. This is the art and science of getting your Web site to pop up first in search engines such as Yahoo! and Google. Typically, this involves making sure that the sorts of words that consumers search on are prominently placed on the site, so that they will be found by the search engines' automatic indexing programs. It requires knowledge of how search engine algorithms work, and the methods people use to conduct their searches.

If you are in your fifties . . . Again, senior career changers are in much the same position as mid-career changers, with perhaps the advantage of more experience. If the system of freelancing, volunteering, or working a bridge job does not work for you, then consider starting your own business. Copywriting will only be a small part of what you do, but you will at least get to exercise your creative bug.

If you are over sixty . . . Very respected authors or those who have risen to the top of their creative professions may be able to find positions as advertising copywriters, or consult for firms dealing with the particular fields with which they are familiar. Still, nothing is impossible. Some agencies may be glad to have your wealth of experience and unique perspective on their side. If you have the means and the drive, consider starting your own business.

Further Resources

Advertising Age and *Adweek* keep you up-to-date with what's going on in the industry. http://adage.com http://www.adweek.com
The Public Relations Society of America is the trade organization for public-relations professionals and individuals who work in advertising. http://www.prsa.org

Graphic Designer or Media Designer

Graphic Designer or Media Designer

Career Compasses

Here's the breakdown of what it takes to become a graphic or media designer.

Relevant Knowledge of the software and other tools you need to do this job, as well as the principles of design (30%)

Caring about the project you're working on invariably produces better results (10%)

Organizational Skills to keep track of what clients want and what your deadlines are (10%)

Communication Skills—in this case an artistic flair and an eye for design, are the most important quality for a graphic or media designer (50%)

Destination: Graphic Designer or Media Designer

Simply put, the job of a graphic designer is to create images and lay out text. While in the past the job was mainly visual, the advent of the World Wide Web and multimedia software has given rise to a new specialty: the *media designer*. The media designer handles not just visual design, but also animation and sound.

Behind this simple explanation is a lot more than meets the eye. The graphic or media designer's main job can be seen as problem solving.

Essential Gear

Here are some of the basic software programs you would need to be familiar with as a graphic designer:

Adobe InDesign: Along with **QuarkXPress**, is one of the two standard layout programs. These are used to design printed materials. It is an enormously powerful program, used to position text and images on a page, design the "flow" and look of the text, adjust colors and contrasts, and export the finished product in a format that's ready to go to the printing press.

Adobe Photoshop: Photoshop is the industry-standard tool for editing photos. Using Photoshop, errors, colors, and shading can be corrected; composite photos can be assembled; backgrounds and lighting can be changed; and things made to look "better than life." Photoshop also has limited text-editing capabilities.

Adobe Illustrator: What Photoshop is to photography, Illustrator is to drawing. An important tool in the graphic designer's arsenal, Illustrator is a sophisticated drawing program that allows you to create charts, graphs, logos, and designs in whatever style you like.

Dreamweaver: Developed by Macromedia and now owned by Adobe, which bought the company in 2005, Dreamweaver is a WYSIWYG ("What You See Is What You Get") program that enables users to create Web pages in a graphical, intuitive way.

Flash: Adobe's animation program. Flash allows you to create surprisingly sophisticated cartoons, animations, and other multimedia in a format that can be read by any modern computer.

How do you present information in a way that is both aesthetic *and* communicates the idea that the client wants to get across? For advertising purposes, the issues get even more complex. What images or ideas does the client who commissioned the advertising campaign wish to project? How do ideas of "branding" and brand identity enter the picture? Is the product classy, cool, sexy, or smart? Is it a product of the future, or retro-hip? A good designer can communicate all this at a glance without using a single word. Instead, he or she uses the timeless principles of design. For instance, a blue background gives an idea of coolness and intelligence, while red is spicy, exciting, and *au courant*.

Likewise for media design, not only color but also such cues as background music, light and shadow, transitions, and the timing of the animation will influence the final product. The media designer's job has elements in common with that of a filmmaker's. In addition, he or she must be technically savvy, knowing what is possible within the limits of the software, budget, and printing process.

While keeping grounded in these principles, graphic and media designers must remain current in their field—not just in terms of software, but also in terms of how society is moving. Fashions and styles change, and clients' (and consumers') needs change with them. Designs, motifs, and color schemes are continuously renewed, and the last thing you want is to look dated! On the other hand, graphic and media designers must know how to go the other way, purposefully recalling an earlier time by using the color palette, fonts, and design choices of that era. For instance, in an advertising campaign that appeals to Baby Boomer nostalgia, a graphic designer might use the colors and typefaces similar to those of the 1950s. Likewise, for rhetorical or humorous purposes, a media designer might purposefully quote a visual from an Orson Welles film or use one of George Lucas' well-known "wipe" transitions from the *Star Wars* films. Such touches can add creativity to the scripts one is given to work with.

Speaking of creativity, finding one's own "voice" and style is extremely important. As a graphic or media designer, one is constantly assaulted with new tools and technologies as well as examples of one's colleagues' work. In the midst of all of this it is very important to keep one's own voice. Creative work that follows the crowd and uses the same modish typeface and color palette as everyone else is not creative at all. Likewise, just because technology makes something possible does not mean you should use it for its own sake. Having an instantly recognizable style of your own is not only important because of intangible ideas of artistic expression; it inevitably creates a better end result and thus makes for happier clients.

The appellation of *graphic-* or *media designer* actually includes a number of specialties. It is entirely possible to make a career in a niche specialty. Possible jobs for graphic and media designers include brand identity developers, who coordinate the visual aspect of a particular brand or company identity; logo designers, who, naturally, design logos; illustrators, who create pictures for products and packaging that communicate ideas, tell a story, or explain how to do something; visual image developers, who edit photography, make 3-D models, or create animations and visuals with sound and motion for the World Wide Web, videos, or CDs; layout artists, who coordinate placement of text and images; Web designers, who design Web sites; and interface designers, who create the buttons and tools users need to interact with a Web site or computer program.

Needless to say, this is a very computer-heavy field. Not only do graphic designers use programs such as QuarkXPress and Adobe's Illustrator and Photoshop to design and lay out their work, but an increasing amount of this work is done exclusively for the World Wide Web. Graphic designers must therefore be up-to-date with computer animation programs such as Adobe's Flash. (See "Essential Gear" for a round-up of some of these computer programs.) Because of this, those working in computers or Web design are in a particularly strong position to transfer to graphic designer careers if their graphic arts skills are up to snuff.

Essential Gear

Resolution. No, not grit and determination. "Resolution" refers to how much information an image carries—that is, how close you can zoom in before things get pixelated. Resolution is often measured in dots per square inch, or *dpi*. High-resolution images (300+ dpi) tend to have larger file sizes. When something with too low of a resolution is printed, the result often seems blurry and out-of-focus. Generally, doing things in higher resolution is better, since you can always save a low-res copy.

While most people see the large firms in New York, San Francisco, and Los Angeles as the centers of design, as of 2006 only 20 percent of firms and 25 percent of workers in the advertising industry lived in New York State or California. According to the U.S. Bureau of Labor Statistics, 1 out of every 4 graphic designers in the United States is self-employed and 9 out of 10 worked in "shops" of 20 people or less. About 23,000 people, or 5 percent of the industry, worked as graphic designers in advertising. They are better paid than the national average, earning a median salary of $41,600 in 2006.

For those wishing to transition to this career, some coursework may be necessary in order to learn the software and establish credentials. There are formal educational programs that can train you as a graphic or media designer, over 250 of which are accredited by the National

Association of Schools of Art and Design. However, an artistic eye and raw talent are things that cannot be taught, only developed, and it is not enough to be simply "artistic." You must be able to clearly communicate ideas in a savvy way. The best thing you can do is to invest in the necessary graphic design software and play around with it until you produce results that you like.

The single most valuable thing a fledgling graphic or media designer possesses is his or her career portfolio. *Portfolio* is a somewhat anachronistic term. Today, one more often gives out samples of one's work burned onto a CD or posts them on the Web; he or she then carries the physical copies from interview to interview in a folder. The portfolio shows potential employers that you are able to communicate ideas clearly and with style. You may want to take the approach suggested in the chapter on copywriters and create a portfolio of mock ads. After all, just because you do not have clients does not mean that you cannot use your creative energies! These should be actual samples of full-production, full-color ads in a variety of formats—whether for magazines, billboards or other media outlets—that prospective employers can download, view, and print out in high resolution.

In becoming a graphic designer, one really needs every advantage one can get. The competition for jobs is quite keen. More people try to enter this field every year than there are open positions. However, the rewards as well as the opportunities for advancement are great. Successful graphic designers can go on to become creative directors, successful freelancers, or even founders of their own firms.

You Are Here

To draw your own future, get an idea of where you stand.

Do you have a background in visual arts, design, layout, or filmmaking? In this case, transitioning to a graphic or media design job should be relatively easy. A certificate course in graphic or media design should help. Also look into volunteer work, freelancing, or doing work for start-ups in your community to build up a portfolio. The essential trick will be gearing your experience toward advertising work.

Notes from the Field

Joe Peacock
Graphic designer
Atlanta, Georgia

What were you doing before you decided to change careers?

Before I got into Web design, I was a poorly motivated retail associate at Wal-Mart. Then the dot-com bubble hit and I moved into Web
development, and, along with it, graphic design. As time moved forward,
I focused less on writing code and more on drawing pretty pictures to
the point where it is all I do now (except play Frisbee with my dogs).

Why did you change your career?

Because writing code [is] only marginally less [unpalatable] than [work-
ing at] Wal-Mart. Drawing pretty pictures is where it is at.

How did you make the transition?

From Web development to graphic design, the transition was gradual. I
started by writing a lot of code, and occasionally creating images to go
in as placeholders. As I began to realize I liked that part better, I sought
avenues that would give me greater control over the look and feel of
an application or entity, until eventually I was doing both the entire
layout/design of a site and the development. Then I began delegating the
development part and held onto the part where I got to draw all day.

What are the keys to success in your new career?

Constantly learning what's new and deciding whether or not it makes
any sense. There are trends in graphic design just like there are trends

Are you a working in a creative industry? Again, you have good odds
of transitioning. The advertising world loves creative people. The limiting factor here is that you will need to prove your visual arts talent
to prospective employers. Again, you should build up your portfolio by
volunteering your services, working on political campaigns, and doing
other jobs you can find that suit you. However, in your situation, going
back to school for a degree program or MFA (master of fine arts) might
strengthen your case even more.

in fashion, or television shows, or anything else. The trick is to always be loyal to your style first, then bring in anything new that seems to fit with it. If the current trend is to slap a gradient on everything, gloss every button, and put "BETA!" in a badge after the logo, figure out what aspects play well with your style (gradients, perhaps) and omit the silly bits (gloss everywhere just to show you know Alpha transparency and curves). Stay modern without becoming a trend. Also, learn something new about your tools every day, even if (especially if) you think you know everything. I've been using Photoshop since version 2.5, and there's not a day that goes by that I do not learn something new about how the tool works or how I can better improve my process with it (a new keyboard shortcut, or learning what sort of interesting new thing you can do with the Warp filter). Lastly, know at the very least Photoshop and Illustrator. Both have their place.

Oh wait, that last one was not lastly, this one is: Print (magazines, postcards, anything on paper) is 1200 dpi, shirts and hats are 300 dpi, and the web is 72 dpi. Do not mix the three up, and for heaven's sake, do not give your printer a stretched-out Web graphic. Always work in a higher resolution than your final output calls for and then downsample when you save for production. You can go down all you like, but like the old man on the side of the road whimsically reminiscing about his life will tell you, you cannot go back.

Are you drawing your own map? In this case, you will have to work twice as hard to convince the creative world that you're an "insider." However, you also have the advantage of being able to let your experience in other fields to work for you. For instance, an accountant transitioning to graphic design might specialize in creating art that shows numerical relations in a graphical way; a college professor who wants to become a media designer might produce animations that explain his or her subject to a lay audience; or an engineer could create schematics that show why one product is better than another.

Navigating the Terrain

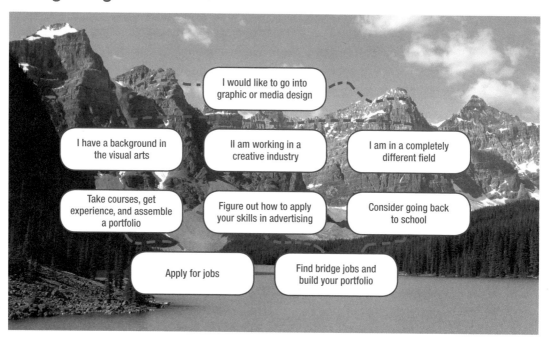

I would like to go into graphic or media design

I have a background in the visual arts

II am working in a creative industry

I am in a completely different field

Take courses, get experience, and assemble a portfolio

Figure out how to apply your skills in advertising

Consider going back to school

Apply for jobs

Find bridge jobs and build your portfolio

Organizing Your Expedition

Before you set out, know where you are going.

Decide on a destination. To become a graphic or media designer, the essential problem is assembling a portfolio. But buying the software and learning is only the first step. Assembling a *quality* portfolio takes more than networking and haranguing people to let you do work for them.

Scout the terrain. What inspires you? What sort of art attracts you? What advertising campaigns stick in your head? What colors do you dream in? What eras have a "look" that evokes a special feeling for you? These are the creative inputs that will guide your graphic design career.

Find the path that's right for you. Now, use your inspiration and your skills. Find those internships, volunteer positions, small businesses, Web sites, and other opportunities to make your vision a reality. Engage in self-promotion by uploading your work to the Web or enter design contests. Most of all, find your "voice" and stick with it.

Landmarks

If you are in your twenties . . . You are in an excellent place to transition to graphic or media design. The advertising industry (and the creative industry in general) loves young creative types. Whether rightly or wrongly, twenty-somethings are seen as being more stylish and with it, as well as better versed in the latest software and computer techniques. You also have the ability to go back to school for your art without facing the age discrimination sometimes encountered by older students. On the other hand, the "hipster ghettos" of New York and San Francisco are filled with twenty-somethings who, convinced they're the "next big thing," spend their lives waiting to be discovered. Make sure to set yourself apart from the crowd by taking risks with your approach to design, studying successful ad campaigns, and mastering the necessary software.

If you are in your thirties or forties . . . While certainly not impossible, it is not as easy to change to a graphic-arts or media-design career at this stage of your life. Like it or not, there is definite age-discrimination. One has to fight against the impression that artists blossom young and the stereotype of the "young genius." You will need to work twice as hard on your portfolio, display double the knowledge, and show work of double the quality. Most of all, try to show that graphic design is a longstanding passion of yours, not a fleeting interest.

If you are in your fifties . . . Senior career changers have similar problems to mid-career changers, with the additional hurdle of needing to show that you are up-to-date with the latest software—or that can you use a computer at all. It is more likely you will find yourself doing graphic or media design as part of your own small advertising agency than going on the job market as a newly-fledged graphic designer.

If you are over sixty . . . Transitioning to graphic or media design is certainly a challenge for second-career starters—which is not to say that it is impossible. You face all the problems of a senior career changer, plus the fact that people will not take you seriously as a "long-term investment." The best solution is to try working pro bono, gradually building a clientele among friends, colleagues, and community members. Seek the input of well-respected workers in closely related fields, such as visual artists or writers, and you will begin to create your own signature "looks" for different ad campaigns.

Further Resources

National Association of Schools of Art and Design Find an accredited program near you. http://nasad.arts-accredit.org

The Art Directors' Club "Creative fuel," critical information and guidance for those interested in internships and careers in advertising. Includes a job board and portfolio-uploading service. http://www.adcglobal.org

Retail Manager

Retail Manager

Career Compasses

Here's the breakdown of what it takes to become a retail manager.

Relevant Knowledge of the industry, the technical aspects of the business, and day-to-day operations (20%)

Organizational Skills to keep a business running, file the necessary paperwork, pay people on time, organize work schedules, etc. (40%)

Communication Skills to lead your team, tell people what needs to be done, and to resolve disputes (20%)

Ability to Manage Stress in this demanding and often hectic job (20%)

Destination: Retail Manager

The manager of a retail store is both the first and the last line in the selling process. Though an increasing amount of business is taking place online, it is within the brick-and-mortar store that customers derive their strongest, sensory experience of a brand. It is here that products have their success or failure. At the same time, the marketing materials and advertising strategies dreamed up in boardrooms and design studios are all aimed at helping you and your sales staff move product. Both parts of the business are interdependent.

Retail stores also have a strong place in shaping brand identity. The entire shopping "experience," from the displays to the music playing over the PA to the way the salespeople look, is part of why people buy certain products. For instance, what does the layout and decoration of Victoria's Secret or Abercrombie and Fitch say about their products? Likewise, a Whole Foods or a Trader Joe's is very different from Wal-Mart or Meijer. Why is this so? Simply put, all of these stores are geared toward attracting a certain type of person. In addition to products, they sell various attributes associated with these products: Victoria's Secret does not sell just women's underthings but also sex appeal; Abercrombie and Fitch sells clothes that convey a sort of mainstream, youthful hipness that is carefully calculated to shock the older generation's morals without too much offense; Whole Foods sells an idea of health and environmental awareness as much as it sells groceries; Trader Joe's sells inexpensive culinary adventures. Wal-Mart and Meijer, on the other hand, are frequented by budget-conscious families with a variety of moral and social beliefs. They are thus careful to be as inoffensive as possible.

The sorts of people who work in these stores are also a reflection of brand strategy, too. Many companies have very carefully articulated dress codes that detail permitted clothing, haircuts, and whether or not body piercings and tattoos may be displayed. Though a store's culture is seldom codified into a hiring manual, it is generally understood that like attracts like. Victoria's Secret salespeople tend to be attractive, but not so attractive that middle-of-the-road consumers are scared away. Abercrombie and Fitch and the Gap also have biases for attractive salespeople, though they tend to employ wholesome-looking, fit, young, "middle American" workers. Whole Foods or Hot Topic employees, however, cultivate a "counterculture" theme and might employ people who wear their hair in dreadlocks or sport Grateful Dead or Tool T-shirts.

All of this is a very deliberate part of marketing. Sociologists refer to the types of products and choices we make in consumption as our *habitus*. For instance, well-educated Northeastern liberals may display their social concern by wearing organically-grown hemp clothing, while suburban soccer moms shop sensibly at Target, and high-powered businessmen indulge in custom-fitted suits. By shopping in these places, we hope, through a type of osmosis, to acquire the attributes that are being used to sell the merchandise. Consumption is thus a form of sympathetic magic.

The sort of retail store you might want to manage thus says a lot about you and your particular habitus. Ask yourself in what kinds of things are you interested. Do you see yourself managing a wine shop? Clothing? Hardware? You will do best if you align your interests and the sort of person you are with what you want to do. Also realize that your retail dreams say a lot about you as a person: do you want to run a chain store, sell a particular brand, or open your own business?

Essential Gear

Here are some of the terms you might encounter as a retail manager.

Rebates: One of many marketing tools that you might use as a retail manager. This is a sales promotion that promises customers money back on their purchase. Rebates have become very popular in recent years because they are a way of discounting the consumer's final price while providing companies accounting benefits and the ability adjust to quickly to market fluctuations. On the other hand, they can be tedious to administer.

POS: Short for "Point of Sale," this is marketing shorthand for a retail location. Thus, cash registers and other day-to-devices are often referred to as "POS hardware." "POS" is a common business term, used for everything from a checkout station to a bartender's post. The essential point is that this is where the money (or plastic) actually changes hands.

Most retail managers start in positions as cashiers, salespersons, and in customer service. While formal education is not a must, experience is. It is also necessary to be familiar with computers to use such things as computerized inventory systems. Some chains and other companies have formal training programs to teach these skills. In a large store, you may be rotated through several departments to learn the ins and outs of the business. Retail managers might also work in tandem with other staff members such as store operations managers, and have other store managers underneath them.

Managing a retail store encompasses numerous responsibilities. You are responsible for the store's overall success and failure. This means keeping the books, ensuring that the store opens and closes on time, ordering and maintaining stock, and preventing theft (often euphemistically referred to as "inventory shrinkage"). You may wind up administering advertising and promotion programs such as rebates. You may also have to set schedules and assign people to specific tasks, such as register, sales floor, inventory, cleaning, and loading or unloading trucks. You have to maintain the brand image of the items you sell. Finally, you are your own human resources department, in charge of hiring and—however difficult—firing.

A retail manager's hours can be long, particularly if he or she owns his or her own business. The hours are particularly long and irregular during sales seasons, such as the Christmas shopping season. According to the U.S. Bureau of Labor Statistics, sales worker supervisors held 2.2 million jobs in 2006. Almost half (44 percent), or just under a million Americans, worked in retail. About 37 percent, or 814,000 people, owned their own businesses. Also according to the U.S. Bureau of Labor Statistics, sales worker supervisors who worked in retail earned a median salary of $33,960, including commissions, as of 2006. The middle 50 percent earned between $26,490 and $44,570 per year, while the lowest 10 percent earned less than $21,420, and the top 10 percent earned more than $59,710. Though the sector's growth is expected to be slow, there is still high job turnover, as this is a high-stress, low-earning, time-intense position. Those with previous sales experience are in a good place to become retail managers. However, it is an easier career to transition into than many others, particularly if you have previous supervisory experience.

You Are Here

Before you can sell your product, you have to get on-track to sell yourself.

Do you have a background in sales? In this case, you are in a good place to become a retail manager. Someone who worked as a traveling salesperson or in corporate sales—in short, someone who understands how things work "upstream" from the store (that is, the corporate decision-making process)—is well-placed to understand what it takes to run a retail store. However, bear in mind that running a store can be very different from selling things to businesses.

Do you have supervisory experience? Having been in a position of responsibility puts you in a strong place to become a retail manager. Nonetheless, this can be a more difficult transition than most. You may not know anything about how the retail business works. Look for ways in which you can bridge the gap between what you know how to do and what you want to do. Many national chains also have manager-training programs.

Do you have more experience with buying things than selling them? Not to worry. The job of retail manager can be learned, though you may have to take some a bridge job or work on the floor for a while. The important thing is not to see retail store management as a step down—particularly if you are taking it out of economic necessity. Another possibility, particularly if you have good business sense and a store of capital, is to open your own store.

Organizing Your Expedition

Before you set out, know where you are going.

Decide on a destination. Look at your résumé. Ignoring such factors as formal education, do you have much experience in retail sales? How about in management? The closer your experience is to what employers are looking for, the easier a time you will have. (If, instead, you would rather work for yourself, see our appendix on "Starting Your Own Business.")

Scout the terrain. Look at the want ads for retail store managers in your neighborhood. What kinds of qualifications are they looking for? Do you have these attributes? If not, what steps might you take to earn them? Do you need to go back to school, take a bridge job, work as a lower-level manager as a while, or even apply for an entry-level position?

Find the path that's right for you. After you have earned the necessary résumé items, begin applying for jobs. Also keep in mind the sort of business you might want to work for—and be sure to project that you are the *kind of person* whose lifestyle and tastes blend with the store's image. Bear in mind that while some stores and chains may hire managers directly, others may only promote internally. You may find yourself stocking shelves and folding sweaters for a while!

Navigating the Terrain

I'd like to become
a retail store manager

Take stock of your résumé

Get a bridge job
and additional training
if necessary

Consider opening your
own business

Apply for jobs

Landmarks

If you are in your twenties . . . You are in a very good position to transfer to a career as a retail manager. If anything, you might be considered somewhat young for this much responsibility. You will probably have to begin in a position of less responsibility. Hard work and dedication will help you advance quickly.

If you are in your thirties or forties . . . Career changers in their thirties and forties are in excellent positions to become retail managers, particularly if they have previous relevant experience. Consider also starting your own business: there is no satisfaction quite like working for yourself.

If you are in your fifties . . . Though employers might be rightfully suspicious of late-career changers giving up professional positions to become retail managers, your organizational skills and sense of responsibility will

Notes from the Field
Shawn Kraft
(Former) Retail manager
Springfield, Missouri

What were you doing before you decided to change careers?

I actually started out in retail, as a manger of two bicycle shops in Chicago, doing a combined total of about $2 million in annual sales. I left that job after accepting the job of General Manager for the Ozark Ducks baseball team in the Frontier League. It enabled me to move back to where I am from, which is Springfield, Missouri. I then left the baseball industry and went back into retail when I bought a used bookstore that has been in business since 1983.

Why did you change your career?

The hours a baseball franchise requires are astronomical. You would have a home stretch that lasted 12 days, 8 A.M. to midnight. It was way too taxing on my family and myself. So, when a business offered itself, I did not hesitate.

stand you in good stead. Your chances are only improved by previous experience. Again, also consider starting your own business.

If you are over sixty . . . Retail management might be a good idea for a second career. Expect, however, to find age discrimination. Make your relevant experience and expectations clear at the outset. Again, you may want to open your own business—though you may also face discrimination when applying for things such as loans and mortgages. Consider selling online as an alternative to opening a brick-and-mortar store.

Further Resources

Be an Effective Retail Manager Career advice from Monster.com.
http://career-advice.monster.com/job-industry-profiles/retail
/management/Be-an-Effective-Retail-Manager/home.aspx
National Retail Federation "The world's largest retail trade association."
http://www.nrf.com

How did you make the transition?

It was a different sort of transition going from high dollar bicycle sales, to operations of a baseball stadium dealing with vendors and coaches/players, to owning a bookstore. That was a much calmer working day. The customers were easy-going and very laid-back. I owned the bookstore for three years and increased sales by over 200 percent via the Internet, using several marketplaces. I sold the bookstore for a very good profit—enough to retire! I now play in the Society for Creative Anachronism full-time and raise my two boys, who are 14 years and 7 months old.

What are the keys to success in your new career?

I believe that the keys to retail success is absolute customer service. Perception of a business and attitude are the only reasons any retail establishment will have repeat business. Even the smallest things like a lawn not mowed, or a ketchup bottle not filled and clean, or a rack that has no product on it will severely hurt a small retail business.

Appendix A

Going Solo: Starting Your Own Business

Starting your own business can be very rewarding—not only in terms of potential financial success, but also in the pleasure derived from building something from the ground up, contributing to the community, being your own boss, and feeling reasonably in control of your fate. However, business ownership carries its own obligations—both in terms of long hours of hard work and new financial and legal responsibilities. If you succeed in growing your business, your responsibilities only increase. Many new business owners come in expecting freedom only to find themselves chained tighter to their desks than ever before. Still, many business owners find greater satisfaction in their career paths than do workers employed by others.

The Internet has also changed the playing field for small business owners, making it easier than ever before to strike out on your own. While small mom-and-pop businesses such as hairdressers and grocery stores have always been part of the economic landscape, the Internet has made reaching and marketing to a niche easier and more profitable. This has made possible a boom in *microbusinesses*. Generally, a microbusiness is considered to have under ten employees. A microbusiness is also sometimes called a *SoHo* for "small office/home office."

The following appendix is intended to explain, in general terms, the steps in launching a small business, no matter whether it is selling your Web-design services or opening a pizzeria with business partners. It will also point out some of the things you will need to bear in mind. Remember also that the particular obligations of your municipality, state, province, or country may vary, and that this is by no means a substitute for doing your own legwork. Further suggested reading is listed at the end.

Crafting a Business Plan

It has often been said that success is 1 percent inspiration and 99 percent perspiration. However, the interface between the two can often be hard to achieve. The first step to taking your idea and making it reality is constructing a viable *business plan*. The purpose of a business plan is to think things all the way through, to make sure your ideas really are profitable, and to figure out the "who, what, when, where, why, and how" of your business. It fills in the details for three areas: your goals, why you think they are attainable, and how you plan to get to there. "You need to know where you're going before you take that first step," says Drew Curtis, successful Internet entrepreneur and founder of the popular newsfilter Fark.com.

Take care in writing your business plan. Generally, these documents contain several parts: An *executive summary* stating the essence of the plan; a *market summary* explaining how a need exists for the product and service you will supply and giving an idea of potential profitability by comparing your business to similar organizations; a *company description* which includes your products and services, why you think your organization will succeed, and any special advantages you have, as well as a description of *organization* and *management*; and your *marketing and sales strategy*. This last item should include market highlights and demographic information and trends that relate to your proposal. Also include a *funding request* for the amount of start-up capital you will need. This is supported by a section on *financials*, or the sort of cash flow you can expect, based on market analysis, projection, and comparison with existing companies. Other needed information, such as personal financial history, résumés, legal documents, or pictures of your product, can be placed in *appendices*.

Use your business plan to get an idea of how much startup money is necessary and to discipline your thinking and challenge your preconceived notions before you develop your cash flow. The business plan will tell you how long it will take before you turn a profit, which in turn is linked to how long it will before you will be able to pay back investors or a bank loan—which is something that anyone supplying you with money will want to know. Even if you are planning to subside on grants or you are not planning on investment or even starting a for-profit company, the discipline imposed by the business plan is still the first step to organizing your venture.

A business plan also gives you a realistic view of your personal financial obligations. How long can you afford to live without regular income? How are you going to afford medical insurance? When will your business begin turning a profit? How much of a profit? Will you need to reinvest your profits in the business, or can you begin living off of them? Proper planning is key to success in any venture.

A final note on business plans: Take into account realistic expected profit minus realistic costs. Many small business owners begin by underestimating start-ups and variable costs (such as electricity bills), and then underpricing their product. This effectively paints them into a corner from which it is hard to make a profit. Allow for realistic market conditions on both the supply and the demand side.

Partnering Up

You should think long and hard about the decision to go into business with a partner (or partners). Whereas other people can bring needed capital, expertise, and labor to a business, they can also be liabilities. The questions you need to ask yourself are:

☞ Will this person be a full and equal partner? In other words, are they able to carry their own weight? Make a full and fair assessment of your potential partner's personality. Going into business with someone who lacks a work ethic, or prefers giving directions to working in the trenches, can be a frustrating experience.

☞ What will they contribute to the business? For instance, a partner may bring in start-up money, facilities, or equipment. However, consider if this is enough of a reason to bring them on board. You may be able to get the same advantages in another way—for instance, renting a garage rather than working out of your partner's. Likewise, doubling skill sets does not always double productivity.

☞ Do they have any liabilities? For instance, if your prospective partner has declared bankruptcy in the past, this can hurt your collective venture's ability to get credit.

☞ Will the profits be able to sustain all the partners? Many start-up ventures do not turn profits immediately, and what little they do produce can be spread thin amongst many partners. Carefully work out the math.

Also bear in mind that going into business together can put a strain on even the best personal relationships. No matter whether it is family, friends, or strangers, keep everything very professional with written agreements regarding these investments. Get everything in writing, and be clear where obligations begin and end. "It's important to go into business with the right people," says Curtis. "If you don't—if it degrades into infighting and petty bickering—it can really go south quickly."

Incorporating. . . or Not

Think long and hard about incorporating. Starting a business often requires a fairly large—and risky—financial investment, which in turn exposes you to personal liability. Furthermore, as your business grows, so does your risk. Incorporating can help you shield yourself from this liability. However, it also has disadvantages.

To begin with, incorporating is not necessary for conducting professional transactions such as obtaining bank accounts and credit. You can do this as a sole proprietor, partnership, or simply by filing a DBA ("doing business as") statement with your local court (also known as "trading as" or an "assumed business name"). The DBA is an accounting entity that facilitates commerce and keeps your business' money separate from your own. However, the DBA does not shield you from responsibility if your business fails. It is entirely possible to ruin your credit, lose your house, and have your other assets seized in the unfortunate event of bankruptcy.

The purpose of incorporating is to shield yourself from personal financial liability. In case the worst happens, only the business' assets can be taken. However, this is not always the best solution. Check your local laws: Many states have laws that prevent a creditor from seizing a non-incorporated small business' assets in case of owner bankruptcy. If you are a corporation, however, the things you use to do business that are owned by the corporation—your office equipment, computers, restaurant refrigerators, and other essential equipment—may be seized by creditors, leaving you no way to work yourself out of debt. This is why it is imperative to consult with a lawyer.

There are other areas in which being a corporation can be an advantage, such as business insurance. Depending on your business needs, insurance can be for a variety of things: malpractice, against delivery failures or spoilage, or liability against defective products or accidents. Furthermore, it is easier to hire employees, obtain credit, and buy health insurance as an organization than as an individual. However, on the downside, corporations are subject to specific and strict laws concerning management and ownership. Again, you should consult with a knowledgeable legal expert.

Among the things you should discuss with your legal expert are the advantages and disadvantages of incorporating in your jurisdiction and which type of incorporation is best for you. The laws on liability and how much of your profit will be taken away in taxes vary widely by state and country. Generally, most small businesses owners opt for *limited liability companies* (LLCs), which gives them more control and a more flexible management structure. (Another possibility is a *limited liability partnership*, or *LLP*, which is especially useful for professionals such as doctors and lawyers.) Finally, there is the *corporation*, which is characterized by transferable ownerships shares, perpetual succession, and, of course, limited liability.

Most small businesses are sole proprietorships, partnerships, or privately-owned corporations. In the past, not many incorporated, since it was necessary to have multiple owners to start a corporation. However, this is changing, since it is now possible in many states for an individual to form a corporation. Note also that the form your business takes is usually not set in stone: A sole proprietorship or partnership can switch to become an LLC as it grows and the risks increase; furthermore, a successful LLC can raise capital by changing its structure to become a corporation and selling stock.

Legal Issues

Many other legal issues besides incorporating (or not) need to be addressed before you start your business. It is impossible to speak directly to every possible business need in this brief appendix, since regulations, licenses, and health and safety codes vary by industry and locality. A restaurant in Manhattan, for instance, has to deal not only with the usual issues such as health inspectors, the state liquor board, but obscure regulations such as New York City's cabaret laws, which prohibit dancing without a license in a place where alcohol is sold. An asbestos-abatement company, on the other hand, has a very different set of standards it has to abide by, including federal regulations. Researching applicable laws is part of starting up any business.

Part of being a wise business owner is knowing when you need help. There is software available for things like bookkeeping, business plans, and Web site creation, but generally, consulting with a knowledgeable professional—an accountant or a lawyer (or both)—is the smartest move. One of the most common mistakes is believing that just because you have expertise in the technical aspects of a certain field, you know all about running a business in that field. Whereas some people may balk at the expense, by suggesting the best way to deal with possible problems, as well as cutting through red tape and seeing possible pitfalls that you may not even have been aware of, such professionals usually more than make up for their cost. After all, they have far more experience at this than does a first-time business owner!

Financial

Another necessary first step in starting a business is obtaining a bank account. However, having the account is not as important as what you do with it. One of the most common problems with small businesses is undercapitalization—especially in brick-and-mortar businesses that sell or make something, rather than service-based businesses. The rule of thumb is that you should have access to money equal to your first year's anticipated profits, plus start-up expenses. (Note that this is not the same as having the money on hand—see the discussion on lines of credit, below.) For instance, if your annual rent, salaries, and equipment will cost $50,000 and you expect $25,000 worth of profit in your first year, you should have access to $75,000 worth of financing.

You need to decide what sort of financing you will need. Small business loans have both advantages and disadvantages. They can provide critical start-up credit, but in order to obtain one, your personal credit will need to be good, and you will, of course, have to pay them off with interest. In general, the more you and your partners put into the business yourselves, the more credit lenders will be willing to extend to you.

Equity can come from your own personal investment, either in cash or an equity loan on your home. You may also want to consider bringing on partners—at least limited financial partners—as a way to cover start-up costs.

It is also worth considering obtaining a line of credit instead of a loan. A loan is taken out all at once, but with a line of credit, you draw on the money as you need it. This both saves you interest payments and means that you have the money you need when you need it. Taking out too large of a loan can be worse than having no money at all! It just sits there collecting interest—or, worse, is spent on something utterly unnecessary—and then is not around when you need it most.

The first five years are the hardest for any business venture; your venture has about double the usual chance of closing in this time (1 out of 6, rather than 1 out of 12). You will probably have to tighten your belt at home, as well as work long hours and keep careful track of your business expenses. Be careful with your money. Do not take unnecessary risks, play it conservatively, and always keep some capital in reserve for emergencies. The hardest part of a new business, of course, is the learning curve of figuring out what, exactly, you need to do to make a profit, and so the best advice is to have plenty of savings—or a job to provide income—while you learn the ropes.

One thing you should not do is count on venture capitalists or "angel investors," that is, businesspeople who make a living investing on other businesses in the hopes that their equity in the company will increase in value. Venture capitalists have gotten something of a reputation as indiscriminate spendthrifts due to some poor choices made during the dot-com boom of the late 1990s, but the fact is that most do not take risks on unproven products. Rather, they are attracted to young companies that have the potential to become regional or national powerhouses and give better-than-average returns. Nor are venture capitalists are endless sources of money; rather, they are savvy businesspeople who are usually attracted to companies that have already experienced a measure of success. Therefore, it is better to rely on your own resources until you have proven your business will work.

Bookkeeping 101

The principles of double-entry bookkeeping have not changed much since its invention in the fifteenth century: one column records debits, and one records credits. The trick is *doing* it. As a small business owner, you need to be disciplined and meticulous at recording your finances. Thankfully, today there is software available that can do everything from tracking payables and receivables to running checks and generating reports.

Honestly ask yourself if you are the sort of person who does a good job keeping track of finances. If you are not, outsource to a bookkeeping company or hire someone to come in once or twice a week to enter invoices and generate checks for you. Also remember that if you have employees or even freelancers, you will have to file tax forms for them at the end of the year.

Another good idea is to have an accountant for your business to handle advice and taxes (federal, state, local, sales tax, etc.). In fact, consulting with an a certified public accountant is a good idea in general, since they are usually aware of laws and rules that you have never even heard of.

Finally, keep your personal and business accounting separate. If your business ever gets audited, the first thing the IRS looks for is personal expenses disguised as business expenses. A good accountant can help you to know what are legitimate business expenses. Everything you take from the business account, such as payroll and reimbursement, must be recorded and classified.

Being an Employer

Know your situation regarding employees. To begin with, if you have any employees, you will need an Employer Identification Number (EIN), also sometimes called a Federal Tax Identification Number. Getting an EIN is simple: You can fill out IRS form SS-4, or complete the process online at http://www.irs.gov.

Having employees carries other responsibilities and legalities with it. To begin with, you will need to pay payroll taxes (otherwise known as "withholding") to cover income tax, unemployment insurance, Social Security, and Medicare, as well as file W-2 and W-4 forms with the government. You will also be required to pay workman's compensation insurance, and will probably also want to find medical insurance. You are also required to abide by your state's nondiscrimination laws. Most states require you to post nondiscrimination and compensation notices in a public area.

Many employers are tempted to unofficially hire workers "off the books." This can have advantages, but can also mean entering a legal gray area. (Note, however, this is different from hiring freelancers, a temp employed by another company, or having a self-employed professional such as an accountant or bookkeeper come in occasionally to provide a service.) It is one thing to hire the neighbor's teenage son on a one-time basis to help you move some boxes, but quite another to have full-time workers working on a cash-and-carry basis. Regular wages must be noted in the accounts, and gaps may be questioned in the event of an audit. If the workers are injured on the job, you are not covered by workman's comp, and are thus vulnerable to lawsuits. If the workers you hired are not legal residents, you can also be liable for civil and criminal penalties. In general, it is best to keep your employees as above-board as possible.

Building a Business

Good business practices are essential to success. First off, do not overextend yourself. Be honest about what you can do and in what time frame. Secondly, be a responsible business owner. In general, if there is a problem, it is best to explain matters honestly to your clients than to leave them without word and wondering. In the former case, there is at least the possibility of salvaging your reputation and credibility.

Most business is still built by personal contacts and word of mouth. It is for this reason that maintaining your list of contacts is an essential practice. Even if a particular contact may not be useful at a particular moment, a future opportunity may present itself—or you may be able to send someone else to them. Networking, in other words, is as important when you are the boss as when you are looking for a job yourself. As the owner of a company, having a network means getting services on better terms, knowing where to go if you need help with a particular problem, or simply being in the right place at the right time to exploit an opportunity. Join professional organizations, the local Chamber of Commerce, clubs and community organizations, and learn to play golf. And remember—never burn a bridge.

Advertising is another way to build a business. Planning an ad campaign is not as difficult as you might think: You probably already know your media market and business community. The trick is applying it. Again, go with your instincts. If you never look twice at your local weekly, other people probably do not, either. If you are in a high-tourist area, though, local tourists maps might be a good way to leverage your marketing dollar. Ask other people in your area or market who have business similar to your own. Depending on your focus, you might want to consider everything from AM radio or local TV networks, to national trade publications, to hiring a PR firm for an all-out blitz. By thinking about these questions, you can spend your advertising dollars most effectively.

Nor should you underestimate the power of using the Internet to build your business. It is a very powerful tool for small businesses, potentially reaching vast numbers of people for relatively little outlay of money. Launching a Web site has become the modern equivalent of hanging out your shingle. Even if you are primarily a brick-and-mortar business, a Web presence can still be an invaluable tool—your store or offices will show up on Google searches, plus customers can find directions to visit you in person. Furthermore, the Internet offers the small-business owner many useful tools. Print and design services, order fulfillment, credit card processing, and networking—both personal and in terms of linking to other sites—are all available online. Web advertising can be useful, too, either by advertising on specialty sites that appeal to your audience, or by using services such as Google AdWords.

Amateurish print ads, TV commercials, and Web sites do not speak well of your business. Good media should be well-designed, well-edited, and well-put together. It need not, however, be expensive. Shop around and, again, use your network.

Flexibility is also important. "In general, a business must adapt to changing conditions, find new customers and find new products or services that customers need when the demand for their older products or services diminishes," says James Peck, a Long Island, New York, entrepreneur. In other words, if your original plan is not working out, or if demand falls, see if you can parlay your experience, skills, and physical plant into meeting other needs. People are not the only ones who can change their path in life; organizations can, too.

A Final Word

In business, as in other areas of life, the advice of more experienced people is essential. "I think it really takes three businesses until you know what you're doing," Drew Curtis confides. "I sure didn't know what I was doing the first time." Listen to what others have to say, no matter whether it is about your Web site or your business plan. One possible solution is seeking out a mentor, someone who has previously launched a successful venture in this field. In any case, before taking any step, ask as many people as many questions as you can. Good advice is invaluable.

Further Resources

American Independent Business Alliance
http://www.amiba.net

American Small Business League
http://www.asbl.com

IRS Small Business and Self-Employed One-Stop Resource
http://www.irs.gov/businesses/small/index.html

The Riley Guide: Steps in Starting Your Own Business
http://www.rileyguide.com/steps.html

Small Business Administration
http://www.sba.gov

Appendix B

Outfitting Yourself for Career Success

As you contemplate a career shift, the first component is to assess your interests. You need to figure out what makes you tick, since there is a far greater chance that you will enjoy and succeed in a career that taps into your passions, inclinations, natural abilities, and training. If you have a general idea of what your interests are, you at least know in which direction you want to travel. You may know you want to simply switch from one sort of nursing to another, or change your life entirely and pursue a dream you have always held. In this case, you can use a specific volume of The Field Guides to Finding a New Career to discover which position to target. If you are unsure of your direction you want to take, well, then the entire scope of the series is open to you! Browse through to see what appeals to you, and see if it matches with your experience and abilities.

The next step you should take is to make a list—do it once in writing—of the skills you have used in a position of responsibility that transfer to the field you are entering. People in charge of interviewing and hiring may well understand that the skills they are looking for in a new hire are used in other fields, but you must spell it out. Most job descriptions are partly a list of skills. Map your experience into that, and very early in your in contacts with a prospective employer explicitly address how you acquired your relevant skills. Pick a relatively unimportant aspect of the job to be your ready answer for where you would look forward to learning within the organization, if this seems essentially correct. When you transfer into a field, softly acknowledge a weakness while relating your readiness to learn, but never lose sight of the value you offer both in your abilities and in the freshness of your perspective.

Energy and Experience

The second component in career-switching success is energy. When Jim Fulmer was 61, he found himself forced to close his piano-repair business. However, he was able to parlay his knowledge of music, pianos, and the musical instruments industry into another job as a sales representative for a large piano manufacturer, and quickly built up a clientele of musical-instrument retailers throughout the East Coast. Fulmer's experience highlights another essential lesson for career-changers: There are plenty of opportunities out there, but jobs will not come to you—especially the career-oriented, well-paying ones. You have to seek them out.

Jim Fulmer's case also illustrates another important point: Former training and experience can be a key to success. "Anyone who has to make a career change in any stage of life has to look at what skills they have acquired but may not be aware of," he says. After all, people can more easily change into careers similar to the ones they are leaving. Training and experience also let you enter with a greater level of seniority, provided you have the other necessary qualifications. For instance, a nurse who is already experienced with administering drugs and their benefits and drawbacks, and who is also graced with the personality and charisma to work with the public, can become a pharmaceutical company sales representative.

Unlock Your Network

The next step toward unlocking the perfect job is networking. The term may be overused, but the idea is as old as civilization. More than other animals, humans need one another. With the Internet and telephone, never in history has it been easier to form (or revive) these essential links. One does not have to gird oneself and attend reunion-type events (though for many this is a fine tactic)—but keep open to opportunities to meet people who may be friendly to you in your field. Ben Franklin understood the principal well—*Poor Richard's Almanac* is something of a treatise on the importance or cultivating what Franklin called "friendships" with benefactors. So follow in the steps of the founding fathers and make friends to get ahead. Remember: helping others feels good; it's often the receiving that gets a little tricky. If you know someone particularly well-connected in your field, consider tapping one or two less important connections first so that you make the most of the important one. As you proceed, keep your strengths foremost in your mind because the glue of commerce is mutual interest.

Eighty percent of job openings are *never advertised*, and, according to the U.S. Bureau of Labor statistics, more than half all employees landed their jobs through networking. Using your personal contacts is far more efficient and effective than trusting your résumé to the Web. On the Web, an employer needs to sort through tens of thousands—or millions—of résumés. When you direct your application to one potential employer, you are directing your inquiry to one person who already knows you. The personal touch is everything: Human beings are social animals, programmed to "read" body language; we are naturally inclined to trust those we meet in person, or who our friends and coworkers have recommended. While Web sites can be useful (for looking through help-wanted ads, for instance), expecting employers to pick you out of the slush pile is as effective as throwing your résumé into a black hole.

Do not send your résumé out just to make yourself feel like you're doing something. The proper way to go about things is to employ discipline and order, and then to apply your charm. Begin your networking efforts by making a list of people you can talk to: colleagues, coworkers, and supervisors, people you have had working relationship with, people from church, athletic teams, political organizations, or other community groups, friends, and relatives. You can expand your networking opportunities by following the suggestions in each chapter of the volumes. Your goal here is not so much to land a job as to expand your possibilities and knowledge: Though the people on your list may not be in the position to help you themselves, they might know someone who is. Meeting with them might also help you understand traits that matter and skills that are valued in the field in which you are interested. Even if the person is a potential employer, it is best to phrase your request as if you were seeking information: "You might not be able to help me, but do you know someone I could talk to who could tell me more about what it is like to work in this field?" Being hungry gives one impression, being desperate quite another.

Keep in mind that networking is a two-way street. If you meet someone who had an opening that is not right for you, but if you could recommend someone else, you have just added to your list two people who will be favorably disposed toward you in the future. Also, bear in mind that *you* can help people in *your* old field, thus adding to your own contacts list.

Networking is especially important to the self-employed or those who start their own businesses. Many people in this situation begin because they either recognize a potential market in a field that they are familiar with, or because full-time employment in this industry is no longer a possibility. Already being well-established in a field can help, but so can asking connections for potential work and generally making it known that you are ready, willing, and able to work. Working your professional connections, in many cases, is the *only* way to establish yourself. A free-lancer's network, in many cases, is like a spider's web. The spider casts out many strands, since he or she never knows which one might land the next meal.

Dial-Up Help

In general, it is better to call contacts directly than to e-mail them. E-mails are easy for busy people to ignore or overlook, even if they do not mean to. Explain your situation as briefly as possible (see the discussion of the "elevator speech"), and ask if you could meet briefly, either at their office or at a neutral place such as a café. (Be sure that you pay the bill in such a situation—it is a way of showing you appreciate their time and effort.) If you get someone's voicemail, give your "elevator speech" and then say you will call back in a few days to follow up—and then do so. If you reach your contact directly and they are too busy to speak or meet with you, make a definite appointment to call back at a later date. Be persistent, but not annoying.

Once you have arranged a meeting, prep yourself. Look at industry publications both in print and online, as well as news reports (here, GoogleNews, which lets you search through online news reports, can be very handy). Having up-to-date information on industry trends shows that you are dedicated, knowledgeable, and focused. Having specific questions on employers and requests for suggestions will set you apart from the rest of the job-hunting pack. Knowing the score—for instance, asking about the value of one sort of certification instead of another—pegs you as an "insider," rather than a dilettante, someone whose name is worth remembering and passing along to a potential employer.

Finally, set the right mood. Here, a little self-hypnosis goes a long way: Look at yourself in the mirror, and tell yourself that you are an enthusiastic, committed professional. Mood affects confidence and performance. Discipline your mind so you keep your perspective and self-respect. Nobody wants to hire someone who comes across as insincere, tells a sob story, or is still in the doldrums of having lost their previous job. At the end of any networking meeting, ask for someone else who might be able to help you in your journey to finding a position in this field, either with information or a potential job opening.

Get a Lift

When you meet with a contact in person (as well as when you run into anyone by chance who may be able to help you), you need an "elevator speech" (so-named because it should be short enough to be delivered during an elevator ride from a ground level to a high floor). This is a summary in which, in less than two minutes, you give them a clear impression of who you are, where you come from, your experience and goals, and why you are on the path you are on. The motto above Plato's Academy holds true: Know Thyself (this is where our Career Compasses and guides will help you). A long and rambling "elevator story" will get you nowhere. Furthermore, be positive: Neither a sad-sack story nor a tirade explaining how everything that went wrong in your old job is someone else's fault will get you anywhere. However, an honest explanation of a less-than-fortunate circumstance, such as a decline in business forcing an office closing, needing to change residence to a place where you are not qualified to work in order to further your spouse's career, or needing to work fewer hours in order to care for an ailing family member, is only honest.

An elevator speech should show 1) you know the business involved; 2) you know the company; 3) you are qualified (here, try to relate your education and work experience to the new situation); and 4) you are goal-oriented, dependable, and hardworking. Striking a balance is important; you want to sound eager, but not overeager. You also want to show a steady work experience, but not that you have been so narrowly focused that you cannot adjust. Most important is emphasizing what you can do for the company. You will be surprised how much information you can include in two minutes. Practice this speech in front of a mirror until you have the key points down perfectly. It should sound natural, and you should come across as friendly, confident, and assertive. Finally, remember eye contact! Good eye contact needs to be part of your presentation, as well as your everyday approach when meeting potential employers and leads.

Get Your Résumé Ready

Everyone knows what a résumé is, but how many of us have really thought about how to put one together? Perhaps no single part of the job search is subject to more anxiety—or myths and misunderstandings—than this 8 ½-by-11-inch sheet of paper.

On the one hand, it is perfectly all right for someone—especially in certain careers, such as academia—to have a résumé that is more than one page. On the other hand, you do not need to tell a future employer *everything.* Trim things down to the most relevant; for a 40-year-old to mention an internship from two decades ago is superfluous. Likewise, do not include irrelevant jobs, lest you seem like a professional career-changer.

Tailor your descriptions of your former employment to the particular position you are seeking. This is not to say you should lie, but do make your experience more appealing. If the job you're looking for involves supervising other people, say if you have done this in the past; if it involves specific knowledge or capabilities, mention that you possess these qualities. In general, try to make your past experience seem as similar to what you are seeking.

The standard advice is to put your Job Objective at the heading of the résumé. An alternative to this is a Professional Summary, which some recruiters and employers prefer. The difference is that a Job Objective mentions the position you are seeking, whereas a Professional Summary mentions your background (e.g. "Objective: To find a position as a sales representative in agribusiness machinery" versus "Experienced sales representative; strengths include background in agribusiness, as well as building team dynamics and market expansion"). Of course, it is easy to come up with two or three versions of the same document for different audiences.

The body of the résumé of an experienced worker varies a lot more than it does at the beginning of your career. You need not put your education or your job experience first; rather, your résumé should emphasize your strengths. If you have a master's degree in a related field, that might want to go before your unrelated job experience. Conversely, if too much education will harm you, you might want to bury that under the section on professional presentations you have given that show how good you are at communicating. If you are currently enrolled in a course or other professional development, be sure to note this (as well as your date of expected graduation). A résumé is a study of blurs, highlights, and jewels. You blur everything you must in order to fit the description of your experience to the job posting. You highlight what is relevant from each and any of your positions worth mentioning. The jewels are the little headers and such—craft them, since they are what is seen first.

You may also want to include professional organizations, work-related achievements, and special abilities, such as your fluency in a foreign language. Also mention your computer software qualifications and capabilities, especially if you are looking for work in a technological field or if you are an older job-seeker who might be perceived as behind the technology curve. Including your interests or family information might or might not be a good idea—no one really cares about your bridge club, and in fact they might worry that your marathon training might take away from your work commitments, but, on the other hand, mentioning your golf handicap or three children might be a good idea if your potential employer is an avid golfer or is a family woman herself.

You can either include your references or simply note, "References available upon request." However, be sure to ask your references' permission to use their names and alert them to the fact that they may be contacted before you include them on your résumé! Be sure to include name, organization, phone number, and e-mail address for each contact.

Today, word processors make it easy to format your résumé. However, beware of prepackaged résumé "wizards"—they do not make you stand out in the crowd. Feel free to strike out on your own, but remember the most important thing in formatting a résumé is consistency. Unless you have a background in typography, do not get too fancy. Finally, be sure to have someone (or several people!) read your résumé over for you.

For more information on résumé writing, check out Web sites such as http://www.resume.monster.com.

Craft Your Cover Letter

It is appropriate to include a cover letter with your résumé. A cover letter lets you convey extra information about yourself that does not fit or is not always appropriate in your résumé, such as why you are no longer working in your original field of employment. You can and should also mention the name of anyone who referred you to the job. You can go into some detail about the reason you are a great match, given the job description. Also address any questions that might be raised in the potential employer's mind (for instance, a gap in employment). Do not, however, ramble on. Your cover letter should stay focused on your goal: To offer a strong, positive impression of yourself and persuade the hiring manager that you are worth an interview. Your cover letter gives you a chance to stand out from the other applicants and sell yourself. In fact, according to a CareerBuilder.com survey, 23 percent of hiring managers say a candidate's ability to relate his or her experience to the job at hand is a top hiring consideration.

Even if you are not a great writer, you can still craft a positive yet concise cover letter in three paragraphs: An introduction containing the specifics of the job you are applying for; a summary of why you are a good fit for the position and what you can do for the company; and a closing with a request for an interview, contact information, and thanks. Remember to vary the structure and tone of your cover letter—do not begin every sentence with "I."

Ace Your Interview

In truth, your interview begins well before you arrive. Be sure to have read up well on the company and its industry. Use Web sites and magazines—http://www.hoovers.com offers free basic business information, and trade magazines deliver both information and a feel for the industries they cover. Also, do not neglect talking to people in your circle who might know about trends in the field. Leave enough time to digest the information so that you can give some independent thought to the company's history and prospects. You don't need to expert when you arrive to be interviewed; but you should be comfortable. The most important element of all is to be poised and relaxed during the interview itself. Preparation and practice can help a lot.

Be sure to develop well-thought-through answers to the following, typical interview openers and standard questsions.

☞ Tell me about yourself. (Do not complain about how unsatisfied you were in your former career, but give a brief summary of your applicable background and interest in the particular job area.) If there is a basis to it, emphasize how much you love to work and how you are a team player.

☞ Why do you want this job? (Speak from the brain, and the heart—of course you want the money, but say a little here about what you find interesting about the field and the company's role in it.)

☞ What makes you a good hire? (Remember here to connect the company's needs and your skill set. Ultimately, your selling points probably come down to one thing: you will make your employer money. You want the prospective hirer to see that your skills are valuable not to the world in general but to this specific company's bottom line. What can you do for them?)

☞ What led you to leave your last job? (If you were fired, still try say something positive, such as, "The business went through a challenging time, and some of the junior marketing people were let go.")

Practice answering these and other questions, and try to be genuinely positive about yourself, and patient with the process. Be secure but not cocky; don't be shy about forcing the focus now and then on positive contributions you have made in your working life—just be specific. As with the elevator speech, practice in front of the mirror.

A couple pleasantries are as natural a way as any to start the actual interview, but observe the interviewer closely for any cues to fall silent and formally begin. Answer directly; when in doubt, finish your phrase and look to the interviewer. Without taking command, you can always ask, "Is there more you would like to know?" Your attentiveness will convey respect. Let your personality show too—a positive attitude and a grounded sense of your abilities will go a long way to getting you considered. During the interview, keep your cell phone off and do not look at your watch. Toward the end of your meeting, you may be asked whether you have any questions. It is a good idea to have one or two in mind. A few examples follow:

☞ "What makes your company special in the field?"

☞ "What do you consider the hardest part of this position?"

☞ "Where are your greatest opportunities for growth?"

☞ "Do you know when you might need anything further from me?"

Leave discussion of terms for future conversations. Make a cordial, smooth exit.

Remember to Follow Up

Send a thank-you note. Employers surveyed by CareerBuilder.com in 2005 said it matters. About 15 percent said they would not hire someone who did not follow up with a thanks. And almost 33 percent would think less of a candidate. The form of the note does not much matter—if you know a manager's preference, use it. Otherwise, just be sure to follow up.

Winning an Offer

A job offer can feel like the culmination of a long and difficult struggle. So naturally, when you hear them, you may be tempted to jump at the offer. Don't. Once an employer wants you, he or she will usually give you a chance to consider the offer. This is the time to discuss terms of employment, such as vacation, overtime, and benefits. A little effort now can be well worth it in the future. Be sure to do a check of prevailing salaries for your field and area before signing on. Web sites for this include Payscale.com, Salary.com, and Salaryexpert.com. If you are thinking about asking for better or different terms from what the prospective employer offered, rest assured—that's how business gets done; and it may just burnish the positive impression you have already made.

Index